My Visit *to* Hell

THE REALITY OF THE UNDERWORLD ANYONE MAY FACE

HS PRESS

My Visit to Hell

to

Hell

**THE REALITY
OF THE
UNDERWORLD
ANYONE
MAY FACE**

EL CANTARE

Ryuho Okawa

HS PRESS

ISBN: 979-8-88737-124-5

First Edition

Contents

CHAPTER ONE

My Visit to Hell
—A journey into today's underworld

CHAPTER TWO

The World of Suffering

—How to get by in a world you cannot control

CHAPTER THREE

Searching for the Starting Point of Enlightenment

—The lifestyle that will decide whether you go to heaven or hell

CHAPTER ONE

My Visit to Hell

—A journey into today's underworld

Recorded in Japanese on November 8, 2006
at Happy Science's General Headquarters in Tokyo.
English translation.

1

11:30 p.m.—The Unexpected Journey into the Spirit World

Initially, I had not planned to give a talk today. My original plan was to read the monthly reports of the Happy Science administration, make decisions about them, and then hold interviews and meetings with top management. So I wanted to get some peaceful sleep last night. But "bad" things particularly tend to occur when I least want them to happen. After I went to bed, I could not fall asleep right away and, while I was struggling to get to sleep, *it* began. I thought, "Ah, here it comes." It started at around 11:30 p.m.

By *it*, I am referring to a journey into the Spirit World. When it starts, I feel that I am pulled strongly into some place and that is how it always begins. It often happens when I least expect it; in fact, it usually happens when I least want it to.

The first journey began at around 11:30 p.m. and finished at around 2:00 a.m. So it lasted for about two and a half hours. I would not have minded if I had been taken to a good place, but unfortunately, I was taken to the world of hell. So, my journey into the Spirit World started with hell this time.

2

A Modern Asura Hell: A World Full of Strife and Destruction

Witnessing the horrific sight of a bomb exploding on a train

The first place I was taken looked very different from the classic image of hell, so I was a little confused as to where I was at first. I suddenly found myself on what seemed to be a train. I could see a European-like landscape out of the window and the passengers looked European as well. As I was looking around, wondering what I was meant to see there, there was an explosion. A bomb exploded inside the train and the Hell of Agonizing Cries unfolded before my very eyes. I had arrived at this hellish scene and watched it all start. I think it was one of the manifestations of the Asura Realm, which is a world of strife and destruction. More specifically, the place seemed like a combination of the Asura Realm and the Hell of Scorching Heat. It felt extremely hot. I felt a blistering heat on my right arm and the sensation stayed with me for quite a while. I was in a hell of scorching heat and agonizing cries.

Besides Europeans, I also saw people who seemed like Muslims, maybe they were Turkish people. Anyhow, I witnessed the horrific sight of a bomb exploding and people getting covered in blood for some time.

The scorching heat of hell is a manifestation of feelings of hatred

After that, I traveled around to numerous other sites of terrorism in the hell realm where horrific incidents kept happening due to terrorist attacks. Similar scenes like these are also unfolding here and there on earth now. In a sense, you can describe them as hell that are currently forming on earth. In this world, buses and trains are being bombed and people are even carrying out suicide bombings in the Middle East.

Likewise, in hell in the Spirit World, spirits with a strong sense of hostility, animosity, hatred, or the desire to commit violence, destruction, or murder come together and repeatedly make similar horrific scenes, although in a slightly different style. These spirits are perhaps still unaware that they are in hell. This is the world I witnessed where I felt the terror of bloodshed and scorching heat.

What I can say from this experience is that words are not enough to save the spirits there. As far as I saw, it seemed impossible to talk to them or have angels speak to them or guide them to heaven. Because of what they experienced on earth, their negative emotions are still raw and require some time to fade away. So they are not calm enough to listen to other people.

They have a strong sense of destruction or violence and are enraged with strong feelings of hatred, wishing to completely destroy their opponent. Their feelings such as wanting to burn their opponent to the ground are what I believe have manifested into the heat in the Hell of Scorching Heat. It was so hot that I felt as though my right arm and shoulder would burn.

Acts of terrorism and war will create hell in the other world

Considering that a life like this could await us in the Spirit World, we must put a stop to acts of murder, violence, and destruction from occurring in this world. What I saw in the Spirit World were similar to terrorist attacks, but in the case of a war [in this world], it will cause more disasters and I presume that their aftereffects [in the Spirit World] would linger for much longer and be more severe.

Given that terrorism can cause horrific situations in the afterlife, it is all the more important that we do not easily approve of starting a war. War immediately creates a realm in hell and deeply embeds hatred in the souls of many. It will create karma that will be carried over numerous reincarnations, leading them to take revenge repeatedly over many lifetimes. The experience of massive trauma in life through destructive acts and murder will have an immense impact on people's souls, and these horrific memories will last for a thousand or two thousand years.

Besides gunpowder and explosives, new weaponry nowadays has enabled humans to carry out various destructive acts and mass slaughter from remote locations without feeling guilty. A person can kill an enormous amount of people with a single push of a button. That is why he or she may not feel so guilty about it, but such kind of acts [terrorism and war] will still create a Hell of Agonizing Cries as a result and create serious karma, both on an individual level and as a group. We must understand this.

When faced with such hellish scenes in the Spirit World, even angels are not able to persuade the spirits there. This made me think that this situation of hell will probably continue for some time and the spirits there will be repeatedly involved in terrorist attacks. This is similar to how the spirits of people who committed suicide continually kill themselves at the same location. The spirits in this Asura Hell experience the same kinds of destructive and murderous acts they did while they were alive. After a while, everything goes back to normal, but then, more destruction occurs. This cycle will continue until all of the spirits there awaken to the spiritual truth and become willing to receive guidance on how to live in the right way.

3

A Modern Hell of Lust: A World Where Women Are Imprisoned in a Western-Style Building

3:00 a.m.—my second visit to the Spirit World

I came back to this world at around 2:00 a.m. but was struggling to get to sleep because I was dealing with the aftereffects of the hell I had just visited. Then, I was pulled into the Spirit World for a second time, at around 3:00 a.m. This time, I found myself in a place that was a little brighter and had colorful scenery. I thought I was in a slightly better place and was relieved at first. But soon, I found out that I was in hell, again.

This time, I arrived at the Realm of Lust, which again looked different from the traditional Realm of Lust. In Happy Science movies, the Realm of Lust is often depicted as the Hell of the Bloody Pond, where people are suffering in a lava-like bath. However, this is a slightly outdated image and the current Realm of Lust does not necessarily take that form. The place I visited had nice scenery, so I initially thought I had arrived at a world similar to the Fairy Realm. I saw a large Western-style building with an orange roof and windows with a Western design. About ten women of different nationalities were living there. At first, I did not recognize that I was in hell, so I was surprised to see that a lot of people from different countries were living there, including European, Indian, Chinese, and Japanese. They all wore different kinds of colorful clothing and had different physical features, and their looks were not bad.

An invisible river stopped me from helping an imprisoned girl escape

As I observed the area for a while, however, I began to sense something odd. It seemed that the women there were imprisoned and unable to escape. They were in a relatively nice-looking Western-style building, but I slowly realized that it was actually a kind of dorm for prostitutes. It was a building to confine women who were working in the sex industry as prostitutes or those who would have been called *geisha* in old times.

Among them was an innocent-looking girl who looked under 20, perhaps 17 or 18 years old. She looked Japanese and was wearing white clothing, which was not a dress but the long undergarment of a Japanese kimono. I thought I might at least be able to help this girl, so I took her hand and tried to get her out of the building and guide her.

The building was surrounded by an open field of flowers and nothing else. But, after going about five to ten meters [15 to 30 feet], there was an invisible, transparent river. It was a type of river that cannot be found in this world. It was transparent. Although we could not see it, the river was surely there, and we got soaked when we tried to cross it. The girl's clothes became so heavily drenched that she almost drowned, so we could not get across to the other side. We made our way back and tried to get out through another route, but our attempt was in vain.

Being chased by a witch,
the mistress of the building

I then tried to help the girl escape through the roof by carrying her with one arm, but as I got closer to the ceiling, it grew taller, which prevented us from escaping through the roof. As I was struggling, other people in the building started to notice that I was trying to take the girl away. Among them was the proprietress, who looked like a witch. I think she was a sorceress or witch, and her face was somewhat familiar. She was a witch with large eyes and long hair, and I could sense that she had an immensely strong willpower. Her role was much like the old mountain hag who appears in Japanese folktales. (She would chase after those who tried to escape from her house.) She seemed to be in her 50s. She was not bad-looking, but she had the scary face of a witch with large eyes and a piercing gaze. I understood that she was the one in charge, the mistress of the house. It was her, the head witch, who was using her willpower or magical power to imprison the women and prevent them from escaping. They were confined inside the building by her willpower.

As I was trying to escape through the ceiling, another woman with long hair in a black Chinese dress came after us. At first, she looked like a normal, pretty woman, but her face turned into something horrific as she chased after us. Her mouth suddenly grew wide up to her ears, her eyes slanted up and gave off an ominous glow, and her fangs grew bigger. The old mountain hag-like witch and other women were also chasing after us, trying to prevent us from escaping. The entrapped women all wanted to escape of course, but since they could not, they would not let any of their fellow captives escape either. Should anybody try, they would drag her back to the building and imprison her.

The women are bound by the fear and oppression they experienced on earth

I did not see any men in the scene, but it was obvious that these women who were being imprisoned were a kind of sex slave. The fact that there is such a realm in the Spirit World means there are many places in Japan as well as the rest of the world where women are treated as commercial sex slaves and unable to escape. For instance, it is reported that some women are brought to Japan from the Philippines or other Southeast Asian countries for such purposes. They are promised good-paying jobs as hostesses and dancers for example, but find themselves being forced into the sex trade to repay their loans. In this way, they are restrained and have no way of escaping. Illegal practices like this occur across the globe, and now these places are like hell to these women, who are held captive and turned into sex slaves. So, in the other world, too, these women seem to be held captive and put under a spell so that they cannot escape. But I am not sure whether they know that they are now in hell.

Anyhow, these women cannot escape no matter how hard they try. They cannot escape through the ceiling or the windows. Even if they are somehow pulled out of the building, an invisible river will block their way. Just as they think they can escape, it turns out they cannot. That is why I struggled to get the young girl out. What made it worse was how I could not speak with this girl, who was about 17 years old, because she just stayed silent. She was a beautiful young woman who resembled the Japanese actress Miho Kanno. In any case, I could not get her out or talk to her. Other women in the building could speak a little, but the girl said nothing at all.

Eventually, after a while of being chased and struggling to escape, the silver cord attached to the top of my head was yanked several times like a puppet string. I was pulled up high above several times and moved up like an astronaut jumping up in outer space. I was pulled up higher and higher until I was drawn back to the earthly world. I believe I went on my second journey at around 3:00 a.m. and returned at around 4:30 a.m. Even after I came back, if I concentrated, I was able to observe the scene through my eyes—I mean my spiritual eyes.

I could not help the spirit of a young girl in the Hell of Lust, just as I could not help the spirits in the Asura Realm that I visited before that. To help the spirits get out of hell, we essentially need to know the circumstances of each spirit, such as how and why they ended up there, and come up with a more personalized approach. Each realm in hell has its own spiritual field, so angels cannot easily guide the spirits out of there; the spirits are under a magical power or spell that prevents them from escaping.

Not all realms of hell are bowl-shaped craters or bloody-pond-like places where there is no way out. The kind of hell I just described also exists. The women there were probably mentally imprisoned by various things during their lives on earth. They may have been indebted, lived in the criminal underworld, traumatized by their parents or siblings, seized by negative feelings they had toward them, or constantly faced threats from others. Because they were imprisoned by fear during their lifetime, even after death, they are still constrained by fear and cannot free themselves from it. This is an example of how fear and oppression people felt when they were alive can strongly constrain their souls and prevent them from being free after death.

Knowledge of the Spirit World and the Truth will give you the power to get out of hell

It is not surprising that such a hell exists. Some women are brought over from foreign countries, forced into illegal labor, and unable to escape from the underground network. Many of them probably end up dying while they are forced to work under terrible conditions. When people die like this, it becomes very difficult to give them appropriate guidance after death. If they find themselves in a modern type of hell like the one I just described, unless they know the truth about the Spirit World or other spiritual truths, they have no way of understanding what exactly is happening to them, why they are there, or how they can get out of there. What is more, they are bound by the spells of witch-like beings, who are more powerful than them, so it is extremely difficult to break away from these spells and get out.

Things will be different if these women find a single light of salvation or connection to the Truth even while living in suffering. For example, even coming across a Happy Science monthly magazine, movie, lecture, or book of Truth while they are alive can help them find a way out of hell after death. Even under restraint, I am sure they have the chance to go outside. At such times, if they attend a gathering at a Happy Science local temple to make some Dharma friends or learn the Truth, there is hope that they will be able to get out of hell after death. But if they die without knowing the Truth, they cannot get out of hell no matter how hard they try because they do not know how. Their mental barriers will be manifested in many ways in hell to restrain them, so they cannot escape. I do not know how long these spirits will be entrapped in this hell, but I assume it will be for quite a long time. Unless something happens to help them escape, these spirits will continue to be bound there. As time passes, some will manage to escape, but there will also be newcomers being dragged down to that hell.

There are probably various kinds of hell that are a little different from the one I saw. All of the spirits trapped there seem to be strongly made to believe that they have no way to live other than their current life. This is why they cannot get out of there. I am speaking from my experience; when I tried to escape with the girl, I could go no further than five to ten meters from the building. The girl would drown in the invisible river, so we were unable to cross it. We could not escape through the ceiling, either. There was absolutely no way out. Such a kind of hell exists, but the spirits trapped there are most likely unaware that they are in hell. They probably just think that they are held captive by a powerful mistress.

After all, knowledge of the Truth is power. Just by knowing the Truth, you will have a chance to get out of hell. This can be explained by the expression, *Sottaku-doji*: for a chick to hatch out of an egg, it has to peck at the eggshell with its beak from the inside while the hen helps it break by pecking from the outside. This means that unless you help yourself by "pecking the eggshell from the inside," you cannot be saved or get out of hell no matter how hard others may try to save you. This was the case with the girl I tried to save; she just kept her silence and did not say a thing. She probably could not understand what was happening to her.

From this experience, I felt once again how extremely important it is for us to spread the Truth to people. You do not need to tell them many things; even a small amount of Truth can help. They just need a connection to the Truth. To that end, we must approach people from all walks of life. This is the feeling I got from the second hell I visited.

4

A Modern Hell of Hungry Ghosts: A World Where Food Is Taken Away by Giants

5:00 a.m.—my third visit to the Spirit World

I was hoping that this journey [the second hell I visited] would be the last one for the night. The first hell was torture by fire and the second was torture by water, where I got "soaked." I wanted these journeys to be over and get some rest as I was going to make important decisions and go to the headquarters to hold meetings today. But contrary to my wishes, I was once again pulled for the third time into the Spirit World at around 5:00 a.m.

This time, it seemed like I was standing on a soccer field. I was clueless as to where I was at first. There were many people there, both adults and children. Shortly after I got there, a giant foreign man, who was over 190 centimeters [about 6 ft. 2 in.] tall and looked Australian appeared in front of me, blocking my view. There was a child nearby, perhaps a fifth or sixth grader, who looked Japanese. The young boy was holding half a piece of toast with something like butter or jam spread on it. Then suddenly, the tall Australian-looking man snatched the toast away from him and ate it. The boy jumped up at the man to try to get it back, but it was in vain. The man was too tall for the boy to reach and he ate the toast that the boy wanted to eat.

As this scene unfolded before my eyes, I could not initially figure out what kind of place I had been brought to. When I looked around, I saw other children having their food snatched away by big adults, such as sandwiches or hamburgers. Some were having their toys snatched away. I could sort of tell that I was in hell, but at first, I could not figure out what type of hell it was. Then I gradually came to realize that it was the Hell of Hungry Ghosts. Like the other two hells I visited beforehand, this hell was also very different from how it is described in classical literature.

Just when the children were about to take the first bite of their food, the big adults snatched it and held it up high out of their reach. Because the children could not reach it, they burst into tears. In this hell, the spirits suffered from not being able to put the food they wanted to eat in their mouth or from having a toy that they were about to play with taken away. No matter how hard the children tried to retrieve their food or toys, they could not do so because the adults were too tall. This is one type of Hell of Hungry Ghosts. Here, the big foreign men were taking the role of ogres, and they were taking away food and toys from children.

Hell inhabited by children who died with regrets after failing to fulfill their wishes

Since there were many children, I observed them to see what common traits these children had. It has traditionally been said that the spirits suffering in the Hell of Hungry Ghosts include many children who died from starvation. But the children I saw this time were different; food was not their real problem. Food was just a symbol or a manifestation of their desire to get something and their situation represented how they could not get what they desperately wanted.

"Who are you?" I asked the young boy in front of me who had his toast snatched away by the large Australian man. The boy answered, "I'm a student studying for an entrance exam." From his age, I could guess that he was preparing to get into junior high school. He was desperate to pass the exam but he failed and was suffering as a result. This was new to me; I had never imagined that children who suffered from failing to pass entrance exams would end up in the Hell of Hungry Ghosts after they died. I thought, "I see. This kind of yearning can also turn people into hungry ghosts."

In this way, these children are very desperate to pass the exam. They study so hard to successfully enter a prestigious junior high school, high school, or university to meet the expectations of their parents. They desperately want to pass the exam and earn that crown. Some children commit suicide because of severe stress or because they lose all hope. Others may die an untimely death from an illness or other unfortunate circumstances. In this way, some children die with regrets after failing to fulfill their wishes. They die without being able to meet their parents' expectations, and nowadays, these children are most likely to have died from suicide. Some children strive so hard under pressure and stress from their parents, but fail to attain their goals, and ultimately die. These children, who die with many regrets for not having attained their goals, find themselves in the modern-type Hell of Hungry Ghosts. In this hell, every child has food, a toy, or something else in their hand, which is a symbol of what they want. These items get taken away by big adults and they burst out crying and screaming. Since this hell was a soccer field-like place, I could tell that a lot of people were there. This was the experience I had.

The large Australian-looking man did not look like a typical ogre. I was somehow able to converse with him in English, so I tried to persuade him. I told the man, "Give that piece of bread back to the child," but he replied, "What right do you have to say that?" So I told him, "I am a sort of judge. Children must be protected, and I must secure children's rights. That is the boy's food, so give it back to him." I spoke to the foreign man this way but he did not listen to me. He just replied, "I've never heard of securing children's rights. And I've never heard of a judge like you." This was another type of hell I visited and I could not settle the problem there, either.

5

The Way of Living that Will Prevent You from Falling into the Three Realms of Hell

Lessons from each realm of hell

The first hell I visited was the Asura Hell which was mixed with the Hell of Scorching Heat. The second hell was a peculiar type of the Hell of Lust, which can be described as the Hell of Lust under imprisonment. The third hell I visited was a modernized version of the Hell of Hungry Ghosts, a manifestation of the unsatisfied desires of children today and their pain of not getting what they want. In old times, it was said that children who died young but could not return to heaven would go to the shores of the River Styx, where they would pile up stones all day long. When their stone towers were stacked up high, ogres would come and smash them and the children would have to start all over again. This is a famous tale told in Mount Osore in Aomori Prefecture, Japan. Nowadays, however, things are different. There is a hell where children are deprived of the items they want. As soon as they are about to bite into their food or play with a toy, they have it taken away. In this Hell of Hungry Ghosts, I saw many lost souls of children. But this hell is still in the shallow area. All three realms I visited are located in a relatively shallow, not-so-deep part of hell.

The first hell relates to violence. It means that violence and murder are definite, physical causes that create hell. So, the first hell teaches us that it is still an important mission for religion to give warnings against violence and harmful acts toward other people, including murder and assaults.

The second hell, of course, relates to the sexual issue between men and women, but it also tells us that to restrain, control, or enslave another human being in an unjust manner—whether it be a man or a woman—is a huge sin. To put others under restraint and control them as if they were slaves, or to use power to ruthlessly suppress, threaten, imprison, or deprive others of their freedom is a grave sin. These acts create hell. So, this hell teaches us that religion has a mission to protect the rights of the oppressed and their hopes to live freely.

The third hell shows us the current state of the world. Now that society has developed significantly, we are living in a magical age where we can get many things. There are abundant material goods, objects, and money, and living has become far more convenient than before. But even when it seems like we can get anything we want, there are still things we cannot get. Because people's desires have also become inflated, sometimes they cannot get what they want or their wishes do not always come true. Once people secure their bare minimum, they become greedy and seek more. They seek something better and want to achieve a higher position. They compete with others and even kick others down to win. As a result of living under excessive expectations and stress, a modern style of hell is unfolding, where the spirits suffer from not being able to get what they want. It is unfolding in a style that is different from how it is traditionally depicted.

To avoid falling into this hell, you can apply the basic principles of Buddhism. Intense competition in this world is one reason people are creating hell. In the business world, for example, people are very competitive and some even use illegal means to get ahead of others. Children are also intensely competing with each other.

Some people create hell because they want to look good, among other reasons. We need to teach these people the meaning of an "it's enough mind"—the way to live in contentment, the Middle Way of life, the right way to live, and the spiritual way of life in which we practice self-reflection and appropriately control our desires. I strongly feel that teaching these things is an important part of our mission.

The importance of teaching people today about the modern types of hell

The conventional realms of hell taught in Buddhism still exist in the modern age, but some of them take very different shapes and forms like the ones I talked about today. If people who do not know about this Spiritual Truth die, end up in the first hell I visited, and get involved in the train explosion, they will most likely think that it is real and believe that they are still alive as human beings. The spirits in the second hell are also most likely unaware that they are in hell. Although they may sense that they are in a strange place, they believe that they are still alive and are locked up and imprisoned somewhere, just like how, during their lifetime, they were taken from their native countries to be confined elsewhere. The spirits in the third hell probably think similarly. A child would not be able to understand that the soccer field—where his piece of toast is taken away as he is about to eat it—is hell. I think it is also difficult to get out of this hell. Children, too, need spiritual knowledge.

All the above are accounts of my visit to these three realms in hell, which are located in a relatively shallow part of hell. I experienced the scenes in full color and they felt quite real. I was able to touch and feel the shape, the temperature, the heat on my body, the vibration of movement, and the coldness. It was certainly different from the usual dream you would have during sleep in that I was brought back to the earthly world by the pulling of the silver cord attached to my physical body. When I faced some kind of crisis, as I said earlier, I was pulled from above and sprung up like Pinocchio on a string. This actually happened several times. It may be similar to diving in water wearing scuba gear and then being pulled up by a rope. I clearly remember all my experiences and they are so vivid that I can explain them in detail.

After visiting the three realms of hell, I felt that there is still so much for us to do as a religion. People today who end up in these newly formed realms of hell after death will probably not be able to recognize that they are in hell, and will not know how to get out of there. I strongly feel that we must sow the seeds of Buddha's Truth in the hearts of many different kinds of people using various modern approaches. We must carry out this activity powerfully, tenaciously, widely, and without giving up. Today was a light talk, but this concludes the story of my visit to hell.

CHAPTER TWO

The World of Suffering

—How to get by in a world you cannot control

Originally recorded in Japanese on February 25, 2022
at the Special Lecture Hall of Happy Science.
English translation.

1

The Problem with Thinking, "As Long as Things Are Good Now, Life Is Good"

Shakyamuni Buddha explored and taught how to be liberated from the world of suffering

Today's lecture is on the topic, "The World of Suffering."

Not many people seem to know this, but if we explain Buddhism in simple words, it is as follows: "Shakyamuni Buddha awakened to the fact that life is full of suffering, explored ways to be liberated from this world of suffering, and then taught them to people." To young people, especially those in their teens or twenties, I feel that this Truth will sound too pessimistic. They will feel that it has no dream or lacks hope and they prefer a more progress-oriented, positive, and brighter view of life. This is how I used to feel as well. I wondered if that was the right way to see life.

Having lived for several decades after that, however, my thoughts have become more in line with Shakyamuni

Buddha's thoughts. Although this depends on how old Buddha was when he taught the teachings, the older I get, the more I generally tend to agree. From this, I think that a large part of the teachings of Shakyamuni Buddha that have been handed down to this day are the ones he taught in his later years.

The complaints young people made in my dream

Shakyamuni Buddha saw this world as a world of suffering. Let me explain what exactly he meant by that.

A few days ago this week, in the early hours of the morning, I had a dream where I was in Kabuki-cho in Shinjuku (Tokyo, Japan). There, I saw young troublemakers who were enjoying the nightlife. They were rebellious, getting involved in fights, and drinking alcohol. I also saw volunteers and police officers who were trying to help these delinquents get back on the right track. Kabuki-cho is a kind of red-light district, where people often hang out, drink alcohol, and stir up trouble. In the dream, I reprimanded the young people, or more like preached to them. It felt like I was there for nearly four hours teaching them why their actions were wrong. I remember the dream very clearly because I just had it earlier this week.

These young people were basically complaining about how they would lose out if they did not enjoy life from a young age and being defiant. They were all saying, "Why is there an age limit to drinking? I don't understand." "What's wrong with men seeking women and women seeking men? What's wrong with skipping school and enjoying ourselves in Kabuki-cho?" "It's nonsense to become a salaried worker. What's in it for me? I don't see any benefit in becoming a company slave." "There's no fun in going to school. Why should I listen to what teachers say? They just try to control us by threatening that if we don't behave, they won't let us advance in education or graduate, and they tell us that we'll fall behind in this society that prioritizes academic background. Why should I listen to them? They are mere teachers. They've only been teaching for decades. They've achieved nothing. So, why should I listen to these people?"

I am sure these youngsters have similar thoughts toward their parents as well. They rebel against their parents and hang out until late at night, although fewer people are able to nowadays because many shops are having to close early due to the coronavirus pandemic (at the time of the lecture). I get a sense that quite a lot of young people in this world are going against living a conventional way of life. They want to know why they have to go to school and do homework when they want to enjoy themselves in a video arcade, or why they have to study after club activities when they want to hang out and get drinks or stay over at their friend's house. Many young people are basically going against the values and rules that have been set by adults.

Of course, they can be defiant if they want to, but as the saying goes, "What goes around comes around." In the long run, they will have to pay the price for what they did. This is the law of cause and effect. Adults often say, "Don't do this" or "Don't do that," but that is because they know that doing them will, in many cases, make you stray from the right track or even ruin you to the point of no return.

Common traits in people who become alcoholics and drug addicts

There is also the issue of drugs such as narcotics and stimulants. In Japan, they are particularly rampant in Shibuya and Shinjuku. Some people sell drugs to make easy money whereas others use them themselves. So, they will need more money and will go on to commit theft, robbery, or other unlawful acts.

People who use these drugs apparently think, "What's wrong with using drugs and stimulants? Doing so may damage my body, but that's none of your business. It's my body. It is up to me to decide what I do with it." These people vent their frustration by drinking alcohol and they also see no problem in doing so with drugs, either.

I have never taken drugs myself, so I do not know how it actually feels, but I have heard and read about what people experience when they do. According to them, drugs, which can be taken through the mouth, by injection, or by snorting them, will make you really high. Apparently, when you are on drugs, you become high and feel good and elated for some time as if you are going wild at a festival at night. That is why people with short-sighted thinking who just live in the moment tend to think, "What's wrong with venting my frustration and getting high on drugs and becoming happy?" Even if others warn them and say, "In five to ten years, your body will pay the price. You may not be able to find a decent job. You may even be arrested by the police and put in jail," people with short-term thinking say, "I get to enjoy the moment so I see nothing wrong with it."

There are all kinds of drugs out there and I am not sure how different they are from each other, but I know that in the area called the Golden Triangle, which includes a part of Thailand, people cultivate opium poppy, among other plants. Whatever the type of drug, it numbs people's senses. The feelings you get from drugs are a little different from alcohol because they make you "trip" or hallucinate. It is said that a psychedelic experience is a little similar to the spiritual experience that one has during religious discipline. So, in that sense, you could say that drugs are a means to leave this world and take your mind off of the issues in this world.

For example, in India, there are many practitioners who do not want to go through the pain of long, orthodox spiritual discipline to attain enlightenment and turn to drugs. They use them in caves alongside the Ganges River. I guess doing so gives them a similar sensation to a spiritual experience. When they use drugs, they gradually lose their senses and become incapable of telling what is reality and what is an illusion. Some of what they see is probably the Spirit World, but others are illusions created from mental confusion. Although their experiences are somewhat related to the Spirit World, I do not think they are connected to the good part of it.

In South America, too, coca leaves are often used. As coca leaves have a numbing, anesthetic effect, they are certainly helpful when it comes to alleviating the pain that patients with terminal illnesses have. But the problem is that, when children and adults casually use coca leaves, they develop an addiction. This is true with Coca-Cola as well. Drinks like Coca-Cola and Pepsi are addictive, and so is coffee, because it contains caffeine which makes you want to keep drinking it.

The question is how much damage these products do to your body if you keep consuming them. Of course, alcohol also has an addictive nature which makes you want to keep drinking it. Tobacco is another addictive product that people often find hard to quit, although fewer people smoke nowadays. It is said that tobacco has a sedative effect and can make you relax when you are stressed out.

Overall, people who are impulsive or who have a narrow view of life tend to become addicted to drugs and alcohol. Usually, these people do not like to face themselves squarely and instead want to escape from reality. They have the urge to escape from society, social obligations, and other responsibilities.

Issues with underage drinking

Smoking tobacco is banned in many places [in Japan], like offices and trains, although it is not illegal to smoke it.

There are other behaviors that are classified as illegal. Some complain about the ban on underage drinking because the level of alcohol tolerance varies from person to person. In Japan, when someone enters a university and joins a club, they are often invited to the welcome party for freshmen where they are pretty much made to drink alcohol despite being only 18 or 19 years old.

(Translator's Note: The legal drinking age in Japan is 20.) Upperclassmen pressure them to drink by saying, "This is our club's rite of passage. We cannot accept you unless you drink it," "I'm offering you a drink, so don't tell me you can't drink." Underage drinking can happen in this way at these parties.

I experienced something similar when I was young. When I entered university, I joined a kendo club and it held a welcome party for the newcomers. I did not think that people under 20 would be drinking, but contrary to my expectations, I was made to drink right away. Because I had never consumed alcohol, I passed out and fell asleep instantly, so I missed out on the curry that was ordered for everyone. I still regret that I missed out on it even though more than 40 years have passed. When I woke up, everyone had already finished their meal. Even though I told them I had not had my meal, they just said, "It's your fault for falling asleep." But I drank because I was made to drink. I only had one or two sake cups, which was enough to put me to sleep. People involved in sports are generally strict and do not accept excuses, and the upperclassmen in the kendo club did not go easy on me, either. I remember to this day how I left the party feeling extremely hungry.

Back when I just started working, I used to decline any drinks I was offered because I knew I could not handle alcohol. But on some occasions, I was more or less made to drink because some of my superiors forced me to. This often put me in difficult situations as I could barely tolerate alcohol.

Some people can hold their drink really well. They have a high tolerance for alcohol in a genetic sense. So the tolerance level depends on each person and you cannot treat everyone in the same way. To use a relative of mine as an example, when my cousin was in elementary school, she could already drink gin or gin and tonic, although I do not know the specifics. When I went to a funeral or memorial service for one of our relatives, I remember seeing her drink a colorless liquid like this one [*pointing at a glass of water on the podium*] during the meal after the ceremony. At the time, I thought she was drinking water. She then said to me, "I can drink it, so you should, too." I took a sip, but my mouth started to burn straight away. I remember rushing outside and drinking a lot of water directly from the tap.

Some people can hold alcohol and some cannot, so it may not be fair to ban alcohol until a certain age for everyone. Even so, the reason why drinking alcohol is restricted up to a certain age is that alcohol is often related to crime and that young people usually have less self-control. Over time, alcohol can make people gradually lose focus on what they ought to do every day and instead make them inclined toward escaping from reality. I believe this is the negative impact of underage drinking.

Although I do not have much professional knowledge of doping, there was an issue at the Olympics recently; a 15-year-old Russian figure skater allegedly took three different types of drugs. Apparently, some drugs numb the physical pain and enhance physical performance. Given everyone is supposed to be competing on equal terms, it would be unfair if she took those drugs. All competitors feel pain as they perform. For example, the Japanese figure skater Yuzuru Hanyu, who injured his legs, must also be enduring pain as he skates. But if he were to take drugs to numb the pain or increase muscle performance, it would give him an advantage over other competitors. That is why the Olympic Committee uniformly bans doping for all athletes. However, because the Russian figure skater in question was 15 years old—an age that still requires supervision—she was exempt from responsibility and was permitted to perform in this year's Olympics (2022). Otherwise, she would have been disqualified. I think this is a tough case to handle. There are various competitive methods that are considered unfair, and in a way, doping is similar to cheating on exams. So when people are expected to compete on an equal footing, factors that lead to unfair competition are considered bad.

The difficulty of getting back on the right track

Going back to the story of the dream I mentioned earlier, I was lecturing young delinquents. I did not know how old they were, but they were skipping school and enjoying themselves in Kabuki-cho. What I sensed from them was that they did not have any sense of responsibility toward their future. They appeared clueless when I asked them, "If you keep living the way you are now, what do you think will become of you in 5, 10, or 20 years?"

What is more, they seemed to think that the way they lived was not a big deal since other people in the same age group, as well as older teens, lived in the same way. Just as how there is a saying, "birds of a feather flock together," those who are alike tend to stick together, so of course, they all want to do similar things. Since everyone around them acts the same, it will not seem like they are doing something wrong. Also, if one of them refuses to do what the other people in the group are doing, he or she will be left out. These types of people usually do not attend school or have run away because they have no place at home, so if they lose their friends as well, they will feel very lonely. This feeling is understandable.

People who continue to go down the wrong path often think they still have a long way to go, but they will gradually get dragged even deeper into the dark side. In most cases, they will end up becoming involved with the yakuza. Illegal activities are often connected to black market trading. To make money, yakuza resort to illegal means such as activities involving things like alcohol, women, gambling, drugs, stimulants, and so on. Yakuza are usually behind those types of illegal activities. In the case of young delinquents, they start by running errands for yakuza and gradually become more deeply involved until they become "professionals" themselves in the end. Once they fall to that level, it becomes extremely difficult for them to leave the world of yakuza and mend their way of life.

Nevertheless, a certain percentage of people previously involved in the criminal world have managed to get back on the right track through Happy Science teachings and become believers. During the early days of Happy Science, for example, our members in Hawaii often visited prisons to convey the Truth, even though I did not tell them to do so. In countries like the United States, many people are arrested and imprisoned for crimes related to illegal substances. My books did not directly deal with drug addiction, but many people recovered from their addiction and managed to rebuild their lives by reading them. In Japan, too, I have heard that our members often donate Happy Science books to inmates. Many of the inmates have strived to rehabilitate and become good human beings after reading them. Of course, many people get back on their feet by reading my books or listening to my lectures before doing things that would put them in jail. In prison, traditional scriptures such as the Bible and Buddhist scriptures are often offered to help inmates rebuild their lives, but I have heard that our books are also being offered to them as modern teachings.

2

Worldly Sufferings that You Cannot Escape From

Poverty in the form of food shortage

• To people living in war zones, an ordinary life without conflict seems like heaven

So why do people engage in unlawful acts or rebel like delinquents? That is ultimately because they are desperate to escape from the sufferings of this world. In many cases, they rebel against their parents, teachers, seniors, or coworkers and commit what are commonly considered wrong acts. These acts generally tend to arise from feelings of wanting to escape the sufferings of this world or escape the sufferings they are facing now.

But suffering is essentially something you cannot escape no matter what you do. Suffering has existed in every age, country, and region. If you live in a war zone, you will probably think that living in peace with your family and working for a company without having to dodge the fires of war would be like living in heaven. You would just want your country to have no cannons and missiles flying over the skies, and no bombs falling on it. I am sure you would want your country to stop fighting or you would want to flee to a country or region where there is no war. But sometimes, a war just happens. This is not something you alone can control; powers beyond your control are usually at work when a war occurs.

•During WWII, people ate sweet potato vines to survive famine

Poverty is another form of suffering that people cannot escape. Of course, there are wealthy people, but in every age and region, there have always been poor people. Poverty is not always about finance, it can go as far as having a lack of food to survive.

People of my generation have probably heard stories from their parents about how they struggled to live during World War II. Their parents witnessed how adults, as well as children, lived back then. My father told me that, in those times, even though farmers grew sweet potatoes, he could not get his hands on them and could only eat the vines of the plants. Also, when they ate rice porridge, they would dilute it by adding lots and lots of water.

My father also told me that during his elementary and junior high school days, he was a little naughty and was preoccupied with stealing sweet potatoes from other people's farms. It was a life-or-death issue for him back then. One time, he was found stealing sweet potatoes from someone's farm and the owner chased after him with a sickle. Apparently, the man chased him from the mountainous area of Kawashima Town, where Special Head Temple Holy Land El Cantare Seitankan is now located, all the way to the foot of the mountain where the train tracks run. Back then, it was hard to even survive each day. It would be impossible to survive on sweet potato vines alone; you would also need to eat the tubers. So, the fact that my father was chased by a man with a sickle back then shows how there were times when even children had to get food through unlawful means. Compared to then, we are now living in times where we can work in an office in a suit, get paid, and eat food we have bought through legitimate means at a supermarket or convenience store. I believe it is a blessing to be able to live in affluent times.

• During wartime, people ate all kinds of creatures

Another episode my father told me was that, during wartime, he caught and ate all kinds of wild creatures, such as lizards, frogs, and snakes. He told me how he caught snakes, peeled off their skin, grilled them like grilled eels, and ate them.

During my childhood, I sometimes spotted toads in our secondary house and, when I caught one, my father skillfully peeled off its skin from its webbed feet. I was quite impressed by his peeling skills. He then chopped off its head and grilled the lower part of the body for me to eat. I tried it and it tasted like chicken breast strips.

In the past, locusts used to be a common food. I have also had them before. As you may already know from reading my other books, our secondary house, which no longer exists, had an old factory on its first floor. It was a factory ruin with broken windows, so many locusts lived in it. When I caught some and brought them home, my father simmered them in soy sauce and made traditional Japanese food, *tsukudani*, for us. Even now, locusts are consumed in many parts of the world that are suffering from food shortages. It seems that about 20 percent of the world's population already consumes insects as a food resource. I, too, have had them before. Thus, food shortage is one form of poverty.

Financial difficulties caused by company bankruptcy and business consolidation

•Many families fell apart after the collapse of the bubble economy in Japan

Lack of money causes all kinds of problems. After the period of high economic growth [in the 1960s], Japan experienced a bubble economy, which collapsed [around 1990] and this caused many companies to go bankrupt. Numerous banks and securities companies that had provided loans to other businesses that went bankrupt also went under and were merged together. A large number of their employees were laid off and many families fell into ruin.

When I was raising my children, I heard that five students in a particular cram school quit in the same month that Yamaichi Securities went bankrupt because their fathers worked there. The company went bankrupt and their fathers could no longer afford to send their children to the cram school that cost tens of thousands of yen per month. From this, we can see that it is a blessing and a luxury for elementary school kids to go to a cram school to prepare for the junior high entrance exam. It was said that to be able to afford the cost of sending your children to a good cram school from elementary school, you needed an annual income of about eight million yen [about US$50,000], which meant you at least had to be a general manager or section chief of a large company. Otherwise, you would be pushing yourself too hard. So, when a company goes under or faces a financial crisis, many children will quit cram school, one after another.

• Some children will develop a victim mentality regardless of their environment

Only when children are no longer able to go to a cram school will they realize for the first time how much of a blessing it was to be able to attend one. While they are attending, they just complain about being made to study all the time—at school during the day and at the cram school at night. Some children develop this kind of victim mentality. They find it a pain going to a cram school. But the children who had to quit because their parents' companies went bankrupt very much envy those who get to go there. Given cram schools provide their students with worksheets containing questions that are predicted to appear on the real exams, preparing for examinations with just school textbooks and a few additional workbooks is very disadvantageous. Naturally, those who attend cram schools are more likely to pass. In Japan, it is almost impossible to get into prestigious schools without going to cram schools. Despite so, some children feel victimized even though they are being given an "elite course" like this. At the same time, there are others who feel victimized for no longer being on that course and finding themselves in a disadvantageous position. So, children will end up feeling the same either way.

People tend to have a subjective view of happiness and unhappiness, or of pleasure and pain, but they need to look around more and be aware of the things that are actually occurring around them—they need to gain a broader perspective. When I was raising my children, it was generally said that, in Tokyo, only one out of six children could apply to prestigious junior high schools. In other words, five out of six children could not. Even so, the total number of children in Tokyo who took the entrance exams for junior high was a few tens of thousands—perhaps 50,000 or so.

Even now, both boys and girls go to cram schools for a few years before taking the exams. Some of them feel victimized for having been forced to study and not able to play with their friends, while others feel victimized for not having been able to get into a good junior high school because their parents could not afford to send them to a cram school.

While some students are busy with studies, others devote themselves to sports like baseball or soccer. In recent years, *shogi* [Japanese chess] has also become popular, so many children attend shogi classes to become professional players, although I am not sure if it is their parents who urge them to do so. Some also go to sumo wrestling classes aiming to become professional sumo wrestlers. Regardless of the field you pursue, it is not easy to fulfill your dream and you cannot achieve it just by wishing for it. You need to go through a lot of tough training. Even so, only a few will be chosen to become successful. This applies to everything, be it in the academic field, sports, or other intellectual activities such as *karuta* [a traditional Japanese card game], shogi, chess, or *go* [a Japanese board game].

All kinds of suffering exist in every age

After World War II, people of the same generation as my father, aunt, and uncle were all struggling to find a way to make a name for themselves. Four of my relatives aspired to become novelists and three of them actually wrote novels when they were young, but only my aunt went on to become a professional writer.

My father also wrote novels. During the weekdays, he went out to work, and on Saturday afternoons and evenings and Sundays, he wrote novels on a small table he had in his bedroom. It was a six-tatami mat room [about 107 sq. ft.], where he laid a *futon* mattress down to sleep. I remember on Sundays, my father would fold up the mattress, place a small table in the corner of the room, and write novels there. He was trying to make something out of his writing. I have read his novels, but from reading them, I got a sense that he did not have many interesting experiences to write about. Although he was not successful in his novels, his works like *haiku* poems—which took less time to write—were often printed in newspapers.

To mention another relative of mine, I had an uncle who started painting in his later years. He worked at the Tokyo Metropolitan Government office. He told me that when he was young, he worked hard to become a novelist by the age of 30, but since he did not have the talent for it, he decided to start drawing instead. He went on to become a member of the Arts Council in Tokyo and his paintings were sold for about 100,000 yen [about US$600] per *gou* [about the size of a postcard]. He managed to reach that level. Even so, when I met him during my university days, he told me how he was no match for other artists, who had studied oil painting or traditional Japanese painting at a younger age at the Tokyo University of the Arts, for example. I remember him saying that they were very talented and that someone like him who had taught himself to draw could never reach their level.

In contrast, my aunt, who was a novelist, was always concerned about her age. She received a "Rookie of the Year Award" when she was over 40 but was embarrassed to have received it at that age. She often said that such awards were meant for younger people, like in their twenties, and that it was embarrassing to be awarded one at her age. She said that receiving those awards at a younger age, not when older, was a sign of becoming a successful novelist.

In the case of my father, since he had to economically support our family with my mother and also take care of two children, he did not have much time to study. He could not afford to buy books to study, so obviously, he was not blessed with the conditions needed to become a professional writer. Novelists often base their stories on their own experiences and will usually run out of ideas after writing one book. That is why they need to do a lot of research to keep writing. For a writer to have enough research materials, they have to give up on other things in their lives. That is why my aunt stayed single and did not have children. If she did have children, she probably could not have kept writing.

Circumstances change with the times, but there are all kinds of suffering that occur at every age, starting with food shortages, the inability to achieve the desired academic results, not making a lot of money, not getting the desired job, losing parents, inheriting debt, bankruptcy, illnesses, and so on. If you perceive this world as a world of suffering, everything can be seen as a form of suffering, so there would be an endless list.

3

The Sufferings of Academic Elites: Facing a Harsh Reality

The suffering that comes with preparing for entrance exams

In urban areas of Japan, children often complain that they are forced to study for entrance exams by their parents and many of them probably acquire a victim mentality, regardless of whether they pass or fail the exams. However, some children cannot go to cram schools even if they want to. A recent Japanese TV drama portrayed that two factors are needed for a child to receive the education necessary to get into a prestigious school: the father's financial power and the mother's craziness. It portrayed that these are the necessary factors to get into prestigious elementary schools, junior high schools, high schools, or universities. Indeed, it is not that easy to succeed in society.

There are cram schools that specialize in preparing children to get into prestigious elementary schools. I feel sorry for kids who are forced to go there at such a young age, but the parents do it because they believe that the older their children get, the more difficult it will be to get into a good school. That is because more people will be applying, so there will be more competition.

Here is something I was told when my children were around the age of entering elementary school. Back then, the current president of IRH Press (at the time of the lecture) was one of my secretaries in our religious headquarters and he took care of my children. One time, he asked for my permission to allow my eldest son and daughter to take the entrance exams for elementary schools. He recommended some schools by showing me the list of their T-scores. The list included Keio Yochisha Elementary School, which was just walking distance from our house. He said, "You need a T-score of 60 to enter Keio Yochisha Elementary School, 70 to enter Keio Junior High School, and 75 to enter Keio High School. To get into Keio University, you need a T-score above 80. The later you take the exam, the more difficult it will be to pass, so I think it will be better for the children to enter Keio Yochisha Elementary School so they can move on to university smoothly." He tried to persuade me like this for two hours.

However, we, the parents, told him, "Is it that difficult to enter Keio University? If they want to go there, all they need to do is to take the entrance exams, right? I don't think it's necessary for our kids to go to Keio from elementary school. Also, if they go there from elementary school, they won't have to take any entrance exams after that, so they might not study hard and instead lack intelligence. Wouldn't that be more concerning?" Maybe we had too much trust and confidence in our children, but this was how we responded. People who attend Keio believe that the earlier they enter it, the greater they are, but in truth, students who enter Keio later on have more academic skills than those who enter it earlier. That is why many of those who enter Keio from an early age often need to study the materials from junior high school again, such as English, after advancing to university.

Also, personal connection often plays a big role in entering Keio. I heard the following stories when my children were preparing for junior high school entrance exams. Former Japanese Prime Minister Kakuei Tanaka asked Keio Junior High School to admit one of the children he had with his mistress. Since Keio could not reject the request of the prime minister, the school accepted the child but later failed him when advancing to Keio High School, saying he did not meet the academic requirements for admission. Around the same time, actor and singer Yuzo Kayama, though I do not know what he is up to recently, had his children attend Keio Yochisha Elementary School. I heard that he even donated hundreds of millions of yen [millions of US dollars] to build a four-way bridge in the large intersection near the school in Hiroo where there had been a lot of accidents. I was quite shocked to hear that he donated that much money to get his children into the school and thought that he was being too spoiling. I myself did not spend that much to take entrance exams, so I could not believe that some parents would go that far. I could hardly believe it because my parents were nothing like him. They would pay the exam fee but would not pay the admission fee for universities other than my first choice.

Another story I have heard was that when former Prime Minister Yasuhiro Nakasone's grandchild took the entrance exam to get into Keio Yochisha Elementary School, Mr. Nakasone waited in front of the school in his car with his secretary until the exam finished. Perhaps it was to put pressure on the school. I assume his grandchild was admitted.

As these examples show, personal connections play a big part in admission to Keio. I was not in favor of using connections in this way and believed that it was important to take exams based on a person's real ability, so I did not allow my children to take the easy route. However, because of this they sometimes complain to me about having to make more effort in their studies.

A high academic background alone will not guarantee you a successful career

Having lived decades of life myself, I can say that life is not so easy and you cannot become successful in society just by entering or graduating from a prestigious school. Even if you have graduated from Keio University, for example, you will not succeed unless you have what it takes to succeed. Just because you are a graduate of Keio

University does not mean you will become the president of a company. If you do not have the required abilities, you will not become one.

The same is true with the graduates of the University of Tokyo; not all graduates go on to become the president of a company. Some of them complain that they suffered because of people's prejudice against graduates of the University of Tokyo. On the other hand, many people probably believe that the reason they have not received a promotion is that they failed to enter the University of Tokyo. However, they must know that a lot of its graduates have actually failed to get promotions. I know of many cases like this. So, I would like people to be aware that not all graduates of the University of Tokyo can go on to become successful. Actually, many of them fail and this is a very painful experience for them. A lot of people tend to make an assumption and say, "He became president because he is a graduate of the University of Tokyo," but that is not entirely true.

I joined a trading company after graduating from the University of Tokyo, but it was not a popular industry among the students there. This was because employees of trading companies are evaluated based on their work performance, meaning their abilities clearly show in the results. In the sales section, the results can be seen in the numbers. The same applies to other lines of work. Whether they made a profit or loss clearly shows in the numbers, as numbers do not lie. In trading companies, those who achieve great results are the ones who are promoted. Graduates of the University of Tokyo generally disliked this kind of evaluation system. That is why they tended to apply for jobs that did not require them to produce tangible results, and the typical place for this is the public office. During the few years of university days, students would study hard to get good grades so that they could land a job at a public office, be on the elite track, and enjoy a stable position until retirement. They made a lot of effort early on, like the hare in the fable, *The Tortoise and the Hare*, to attain this kind of career. The next popular career path was to find a job at a company where many senior graduates of the University of Tokyo were working because their promotion would be guaranteed in a workplace like that. Thus, for graduates of the University of Tokyo, the worst career choice was to join a company that required them to demonstrate their abilities through competition with others.

Some elite employees fall from grace because of issues with interpersonal relationships and blunders at work

When I first joined a trading company, I noticed a strange man in the office, who was probably in his early 50s but looked much older than that. He wore dark-shaded glasses similar to sunglasses and went around like this [*swinging the body sideways*] distributing postal items on people's desks. I found it strange that the company hired someone like him. One day, my superior told me, "Oh, he is a graduate of the University of Tokyo, just like you. He used to be among the elites when he first started working, but now, after 30 years, he ended up like that." The man did not have a job title and was working as the company's "mailman" to receive a salary until retirement. He was there just to distribute incoming mail to different sections. My superior then continued, "He graduated from the Faculty of Law like you did. You may be considered elite now, but you could end up like him in 30 years, so be careful. There are usually two reasons why elites end up like that: one is issues with interpersonal relationships, which is usually the major reason. The other is, of course, making blunders at work, more specifically in sales." So, there was a man like him at my workplace.

The same can happen in public offices. Not everyone there is on a smooth track to promotion. Every year, public offices usually hire 20 new graduates, but only about four of them will be promoted to director, and of those, only one person, or even none, will be promoted to vice-minister. Some of them will change careers once they realize they have no hope of getting a promotion and there were even those who committed suicide by jumping out of the window. So, their future is not always bright.

Regardless of the career you choose to pursue, there will always be painful experiences. Working at a public office is also tough and pretty much physical labor. It is said that when public officers are transferred overseas, they can work at a slower pace, but when they are working in Japan, in places like the Ministry of Finance, they often work until 12:00 a.m. or even 3:00 a.m. Even if they get married, they cannot go home for days, so many soon end up getting a divorce. I heard that in some sections, people have either filed for a divorce or committed suicide in the worst-case scenario.

Even the graduates of a top-flight university need to make efforts to become successful

Life is not that easy and success does not just fall from the sky. There are many extraordinary success stories in society that say, "If you do this, you will be successful." These stories may be true from a broader perspective and some of your acquaintances might have become successful with such methods. However, that is not to say that you, too, will be successful.

In Happy Science, for example, it seems that graduates from Waseda University tend to be promoted to higher positions, like the current chairperson; this has been the case since the early days. This may be because several chairpersons in the past were also from Waseda University. But just because you graduated from Waseda University does not mean you will definitely attain a high position. About 10,000 students graduate from Waseda University every year and they go on to work in many different kinds of workplaces. Some of them will be successful while others will not. The chances of them becoming successful are as good as finding ginkgo nuts under dead ginkgo leaves (a Japanese idiom meaning the chances are slim). In the same way that fortune telling does not always come true, you never know who is going to succeed and who is not.

As far as I have observed, the common traits of Waseda graduates are that they have a good degree of intellect, good enough stamina, and good enough perseverance to do simple tasks that others would not want to do. In the field of religion, these traits probably work to their advantage. In comparison, Keio graduates are a little short of the perseverance needed to do trivial work and tend to behave like aristocrats. As newbies, they are a little snobby and hard to work with as subordinates. In the case of graduates of the University of Tokyo, it depends on each person. In general, they lack societal knowledge as a result of only having learned academic knowledge and not practical knowledge. They will only have studied academic materials and have general knowledge of the liberal arts. For example, if they had studied practical English, they could go overseas to work right after entering a company. But instead of teaching practical English, the professors at the University of Tokyo often start by teaching Shakespeare and then move on to reading an English classic that is at least a century old. This is because the professors are usually doing research on classical literature themselves. To save the time and energy required in making new study materials, they teach the book they are trying to translate or are researching at the time. Naturally, the students who learned classical English cannot speak English at work because what they learned at university is completely different from the practical English used in business. No matter how well they can translate Shakespeare's plays, they will not be able to speak useful English. This is what I learned from my own experience. I assume that the graduates of the University of Tokyo who went on to become successful were either lucky enough to get on the fast track to promotion or have made an active effort to study other things and accumulate experiences on their own after graduation.

Religion is especially unfit for graduates of the University of Tokyo. Some of its graduates have become Happy Science staff members and are still working here and I think these people have probably made a lot of effort to be where they are. Among those graduates, the friendly ones will serve for a long time, while humble and persistent ones will have their efforts gradually recognized after 10 or 20 years. But those who are overconfident and have quickly become conceited [*gesturing having a long nose like a tengu*] will often be deemed useless in the first few years. There are also those who become too strict with their subordinates after attaining a management position and are shunned by their subordinates. So, as far as I have observed, many of them fail to become successful. The University of Tokyo aims to produce people who will go on to become successful in this earthly world, so I do not think that it is a suitable school for those who aspire to become successful in religion, which deals with other-worldly matters.

Even religious leaders need the basic work skills that are usually required in society

I, too, studied at the University of Tokyo, but what stand me in good stead as a religious leader are the things I studied outside of the university curriculum. I studied various topics including religious knowledge on my own, and this store of knowledge serves me greatly in my current work. Most of the things I studied at the university to gain credits are useless for my work. Although they helped me a little to understand the system and mechanism of work in general society and raised my awareness, they were not helpful for me in becoming a religious leader.

To work in religion, it is certainly better to have a literary background, but that knowledge is not enough when doing administrative work. You also need to have the basic work skills that are generally required in society, such as the ability to do work with accuracy and speed, and to make sound judgments. Those who have read a lot of classics or Greek philosophy, for example, may be attracted to working in religion because these types of literature are somewhat similar to religious Truths. But when they become Happy Science staff and are assigned to our local branches, they may turn out to be very slow at their work. It is unfortunate, but these things can happen.

There is a similar issue with English skills. Some people are proficient in practical English as a second language, but that does not necessarily mean they can preach religious Truth in English. No matter how smooth their

English is, if they use business-like English that is used, for example, in contracts, they cannot move people's hearts. You cannot persuade people to join Happy Science with that kind of English. Our staff members need to acquire the speaking skills that will inspire people spiritually and make them want to believe in our religion. This is an ability that can be explored endlessly, and you need to study and research it. It is difficult to know what kinds of English words or expressions move people's hearts. I myself am still exploring this. I believe that inspiring English is different from what is generally called "good" English. Unless you use words and expressions that touch people's hearts and emotions, you cannot move them to tears. Unfortunately, logical English itself will not move people. Rather, even if you speak broken English, if you can speak words that strike people's hearts, you can surely inspire people to join Happy Science. It requires a lot of study and research to be able to do this. It really is not easy to succeed in this world.

4

The Four Pains Taught by Shakyamuni Buddha Still Apply Today

The pain of aging

If I were to use technical terms, the world of suffering is the world of the Four Pains and the Eight Pains. This is actually what Shakyamuni Buddha taught. The Four Pains are the pains of Birth, Aging, Illness, and Death.

You have probably forgotten the pain of being born, but there is also the pain of aging, which I, myself, have been feeling deeply as I grow older. Before giving this lecture, I went to see the Second Angel Shoja [a day nursery run by Happy Science], which was recently completed. Before going there, I watched a video of the lecture I gave in Brazil Shoshinkan 12 years ago in 2010. It took over 24 hours—nearly 30 hours—to travel from Japan to Brazil, and I arrived there a little before noon. That day, I was quite hyped up. Since I was so excited and could not rest, and also because about 200 volunteer members had already gathered at Brazil Shoshinkan, I thought I should not waste the opportunity. So, I gave my very first lecture of about 60 minutes. Back then, I was a little slimmer than I am now and obviously much younger, which makes me a little sad now. Since it was 12 years ago, I looked much younger, indeed, and more high-spirited, which made me feel a little envious of my younger self. Being able to give a lecture right after almost 30 hours of flying meant that I really was full of vitality.

There certainly is the pain that comes with age. As you get older, it gets tougher and tougher to fight against this pain year after year. I believe I still have the stamina of a man in his 40s, but I can no longer do demanding sports or exercises like I used to do in my younger days.

On a positive note, fortunately, the brain does not deteriorate so easily as long as you keep training it. Most people of my generation are in their retirement age, so many of them have left their companies or public offices. I, on the other hand, have been continuing to study. In terms of my intellectual ability, I am now quicker at everything I do compared to when I was young, thanks to my accumulated knowledge. When I was young, I used to think I was a little slow on the uptake, but now, I have gotten quicker. This is probably because I am more knowledgeable now. I often find that I have already studied the things others think of studying from now on. I already studied them when I was younger, went over them in middle age, and then reviewed them again in my later years, which means it would be my third time studying them. That is why I am much quicker now. While the brain also ages, I feel I am delaying mine from deteriorating by training it.

I remember, in the early 1990s when I was around 35 years old, I used to give lectures 18.8 times a year on average, according to what the then-chairperson calculated. I now give about 180 lectures a year on average, which is 10 times more. However, I doubt I could have given 180 lectures back when I was 35 years old. That is because I did not have enough material to give that many lectures. If I had given 180 lectures, I would have been left with nothing to talk about and the content of my lectures would have been quite empty. Considering the amount I studied, my vitality, and my social recognition, 18 lectures a year was probably the most I could give in those days.

Studying to create the foundation of our organization was very taxing work

When we started building our Head Temples, this time, the construction costs weighed heavily on us. To cover the costs, our executives expected me to work harder and give more lectures. In reality, however, I could not give lectures as often and eventually reached the point where I could only give two or three lectures a year. Actually, I was mainly focused on doing administrative work in those days. More specifically, I was giving instructions on how our General Affairs Division and Accounting Division should operate, or how to promote missionary work and assess our achievements.

One time, I discovered that our accounts were settled separately between our headquarters and our branch offices. It was unbelievable and shocking. So, I even had to teach our staff the kind of work I used to do when I was working for a trading company. Although I had hired people who used to work in the finance industry, no one had the experience of assessing the finances of an entire organization like I used to do. They had only worked within their section so they could not think about where their work stood in relation to the entire organization. I was shocked to discover this fact.

The then-general manager of our Finance Division used to be a branch manager of a regional bank, but even someone like him could not grasp the financial situation of our entire organization. He just received the reports that came from our Missionary Promotion Division, which is now renamed the El Cantare-Belief Promotion Division. Although he learned about the amount of donations made at local branches or how many books were sold, he did not check the bank account to see whether the reported payment was actually made. So there was no coordination within the organization. Since the prospective donation or sales was considered actual income, we sometimes did not have the amount of money we expected to receive in our bank account. I was so frightened by this fact. I could not believe the situation back then. As the Master of Happy Science, I had to take care of the organization at this level of detail. We were still at this level in our fourth or fifth year, so there was no way I could give public lectures; I had to teach my staff how to do their work.

What is more, since our branch managers did not know what to talk about to our believers, I had to create materials to help them as well. At the height of this, there was a time when I would also give two lectures a day at our general headquarters. Back then, our monthly magazine used to print a transcript of my lectures, which were about 30 minutes long. I recorded them at our headquarters to show our believers later. After I gave the lecture, I would then give an explanation of it for about 90 minutes for the sake of our Education and Training Division. So, I would give a lecture for 30 minutes and then give another lecture right after for about an hour and a half to explain it further. Our staff in the Education and Training Division would then create a summary of my additional explanation and haughtily send it to our branch managers. Because of this workload, my spiritual energy was drained out and so I could not get my hands on my main work. Happy Science was still an "amateur" organization back then. In the same way that an entrepreneur must be able to do everything himself, a founder of a religion also has to be almighty and capable of everything.

It is very tough when you are required to do everything yourself. While I had no problem dealing with the things I knew about, I had to study or re-study the things I did not know about or could not do. I had to cover everything, so this was truly taxing for me.

In terms of studying, it was tougher than what I had to do during my student days. Since I was studying so earnestly, my ex-wife said that it looked much tougher than studying for entrance exams. It was indeed true. She said, "No one would study this much even for entrance exams," as if it were of no concern to her. The amount of studying required to continuously give lectures as well as manage an organization was extensive and taxing. It was far more strenuous than studying to just earn my own salary; that would have been much easier. But seeing our situation, I had no choice but to do it. I put all my effort into studying and even reading through encyclopedias and dictionaries. So indeed, it was tougher than studying for entrance exams. Not only did I have to make time to study, but I had to make it seem as though I was working, and not just studying so no one would complain. So, it was very difficult to manage my time. In this way, Happy Science went through difficult times.

We had to deal with the mass media, too. Some former Happy Science staff members who were fired, or executives who were fired for their incompetence, went to weekly magazines to sell stories. It was something Judas would do. They would sell gossipy stories, which would be turned into articles. Some former staff members tried to take revenge in this way for having been fired as if to show us what they were capable of. We had to deal with these problems too, so I had to teach our staff how to fight back. At times, I even had to teach our lawyers how to debate and fight in court, which was also taxing. Although I had finished studying law at university, I had to study it all over again. Thus, I had to be almighty and be capable of everything. I also had to accumulate a stock of knowledge in advance and establish the foundation of our organization so it could be maintained in the future. This was indeed very strenuous work.

The pains that young people also experience

The next of the Four Pains is the pain of illness, which is something I have experienced and have talked about in many lectures. Then, there is the pain of death. I believe this is a topic I need to talk about in more detail in my later teachings. Death is a serious matter for older people, so I need to give more lectures about the world after death and how to prepare oneself for death.

Besides the Four Pains, there are also other pains, such as the pain of meeting people you dislike and the pain of parting from the people you love. These should be relevant to young people as well because these experiences are inevitable if you have lived for some decades. In many cases, even among your acquaintances or friends, those you find nice tend to die early while those you despise and wish would die soon—which I should not say as a religious leader—do not and rather tend to live for a long time. Unfortunately, it is often the good-hearted people who die early or face misfortune. As you age, you will have more experiences of parting from your loved ones and meeting people you hate or that hate you.

In addition to these pains, there is the pain of having worldly delusions that come from the five senses. Young people especially are at the mercy of this pain; the same goes for the young people I saw in my dream of Kabuki-cho I mentioned at the beginning of this lecture. In a nutshell, it is the suffering caused by desires that arise from what you perceive with your eyes, ears, nose, tongue, and your physical body, such as your hands. These worldly delusions are basically the desires to live. They are the necessary desires for living creatures to grow and sustain themselves in this world, which include desires for food, sex, and sleep. There is also the desire to survive, which is something we particularly see in animals. In the animal kingdom, the weak are easily preyed upon and eaten. So, animals need the strength to fight even against humans so as not to be caught and consumed.

These desires become stronger as you live, but when you are young, they are very difficult to restrain, which is why you suffer. For example, young people have big appetites, so they eat a lot. This means they are full of energy. If they put that energy to good use, there is no problem, but if they are told to keep quiet or sit still, they will probably go mad. That is why they try to release their energy and use it on other activities, which will sometimes cause trouble for others.

Young salaried workers, for instance, consume more than 3,000 kcal by eating and drinking alcohol; this is an excessive amount of calories. That is why some of them will expend this energy by playing sports while others will engage in sexual activities. If the latter people find a good partner, they may be able to lead a successful life, but if they are caught up in a troublesome relationship, they could become unhappy. Being consumed by this single desire or worldly delusion can change your life for the worse.

Some people may blame their parents for their unhappiness and complain a lot saying, "My parents were bad at parenting," "They neglected me," "They didn't take good care of me," or "They didn't give me enough allowance." But these people will eventually become parents themselves. Some do so by getting involved in a physical relationship at an early stage and unexpectedly having children. As a result, they cannot take responsibility and end up neglecting their children and putting them in worse situations than the environment they were brought up in. These neglected children may then become rebels, delinquents, or cause social issues or trouble in society, only to be put under the care of other people. In this way, as a result of living at the mercy of worldly desires, young people often end up burdening others.

Having said this, however, young people cannot put a stop to their worldly desires no matter how much they are told to do so. Just as a person cannot stop themselves from being hungry, they cannot restrain their desires. When you are starving and devouring food, you cannot stop yourself halfway, even if you are told to. In the same way, young people cannot put a stop to their sexual desires. Since they cannot be stopped, I can only hope that they will at least acquire the ability to think rationally.

To do so, they need to know what kind of situations other people have failed or succeeded in. They can learn this by observing people in society, reading weekly magazines or newspapers, or watching TV; they can learn through various outlets. They should study others and make notes like, "People will end up like this by doing such and such things, so I should be careful not to make the same mistakes," or "This person became successful because of these qualities." Young people need to study other people in this way, take their own personalities into account, and strive to make rational decisions. But I also know that they will not listen to me no matter how much I tell them.

The reason parents lecture their children is to prevent them from making the same mistakes they did, as they, too, made a lot of blunders and went through painful experiences when they were young. This is usually why parents warn their children. At times, they may be referring to the failures of their coworkers or classmates that they have seen. But in most cases, children do not understand the concerns their parents have for them.

5

The Pain that Comes with Success

The pain of the privileged class

Another pain is the pain of not getting what you want. I do not think anyone can escape this pain. There is no such thing as a perfect environment that satisfies you completely, no matter how hard you may try to attain it. This is true in any job you do or in any family or country you are born into.

Let me give you an example. Based on the Constitution of Japan, all Japanese citizens are equal. Article 14 dismisses aristocracy and guarantees equality, with one exception: the imperial family. The very first article of the Japanese Constitution defines the emperor, and there is also a law that only applies to the imperial family called the Imperial Household Law. They are treated differently from ordinary Japanese people; they only have a first name and not a family name, or you could say that their family name is "Japan."

For a long time, no one from the imperial family had ever taken school entrance exams. It was only recently that one of the imperial family members—I am not sure if he will become the successor or not—entered a state-funded high school by taking an entrance exam, perhaps thanks to an arrangement made between the schools involved. This was the first case of a member of the imperial family taking an entrance exam. Usually, the imperial family members cannot attend cram schools and it would cause problems if their scores were posted on the wall of the cram school, saying, "Prince X scored Y points on a test and ranked Z." The cram school would also be in trouble because the imperial family members are always accompanied by the police or chamberlains.

The imperial family is considered noble by the public, but nowadays its young members tend to think about how to leave the imperial family. First, the young princes and princesses will think of ways to avoid enrolling in Gakushuin, a private school that was originally created for imperial family members. They try hard to find ways to enjoy themselves by going to a different school and escaping the eyes of undercover police officers. Going abroad is a good opportunity for that, so they are eager to study abroad. If they have to go to a Japanese university, they think of going to one with less supervision. In this way, the imperial family is becoming unstable now.

You may think that those in a privileged class are blessed, but even they are not entirely satisfied. They want to enjoy freedom like ordinary people and complain that they do not have basic human rights. As they were criticized by weekly magazines, they went as far as to explain how unfairly they were treated compared to other citizens. But in fact, they are different from ordinary citizens in that they are an exception to the rule in the Constitution of Japan. Although they have a duty to pay taxes, they are not defined as normal Japanese citizens.

As a side note, whether their assets are private or public is really unclear. They live in the Imperial Palace located in the middle of Marunouchi in central Tokyo. I do not know how much the price would be if they were to sell their palace; it would probably be tremendously high because its grounds are big enough to contain many high-rise buildings. Calculating the potential price would be considered something like lese-majesty, so I do not think anyone has done it; at least, I have never seen one. I once read that the king of Thailand has assets of 4 trillion yen [about US$25 billion]. But no one in Thailand criticizes the king for that because anyone who badmouths him will be arrested for lese-majesty. So, the king of Thailand is protected by lese-majesty law. Japan, on the other hand, no longer has such a law, so the weekly magazines are free to criticize the imperial family and when they do, the young imperial family members make a fuss saying, "We have no freedom." In prison, criminals are deprived of freedom, and so are the imperial family in the Imperial Palace, just in different ways. Nevertheless, they both suffer from not getting what they want.

Thus, members of the imperial family also experience the pain of not getting what they want. That is why young imperial family members tend to say, "What's wrong with marrying someone I love? Why does everyone oppose it? I don't get it." One of the princesses actually left the imperial family to live in New York just after getting married. Likewise, in the past, when Empress Masako was a candidate to be the wife of the then-Crown Prince, her family lineage was investigated thoroughly. I remember that, when it was found that her grandfather's company named Chisso once caused water pollution when he was president, some scholars discussed whether this should be taken up as an issue. It must have been quite painful to be considered responsible for things to that extent. Similarly, when Empress Emerita Michiko entered the imperial family, her ladies-in-waiting teased her by calling her "the daughter of a miller" because her father was the president of Nisshin Seifun [a major Japanese flour milling company]. When she cooked, she was looked down on as a civilian, and when she breastfed her own baby, she was scorned as low class. She was told that breastfeeding is a wet nurse's job. I heard that she experienced difficult times like this in the imperial household.

The higher your status, the more criticism and attacks you will receive

There is no end to the pain of not getting what you want. Whoever you are, be it a king, a president of a country, a pauper, or a beggar, you can never escape this pain.

Everyone experiences this pain. For instance, although Mr. Putin can launch an attack on Ukraine, he cannot put a stop to the accusations coming from the media around the world. As the president, I am sure he does not want to read them or let others read them, but he cannot stop people from making accusations. Obviously, he cannot conduct an airstrike on all the media companies. So, even he cannot make everything go the way he wants.

The older you get, the more things there will be that you cannot control. The higher your social status, the more criticisms and attacks you will receive. At times, you must accept these criticisms to some extent, and at other times, you must fight back. It is indeed difficult to make adjustments by determining what to accept and what to fight back at.

In this world, there is freedom of speech, so of course, some people will criticize, while others will become the target of criticism. Sometimes, you can logically criticize other people, but usually, as you become more influential, you will be criticized more than you criticize them and refrain from fighting back. Once you become prime minister, for example, you will suddenly see many articles criticizing you, but you will remain silent most of the time. Some criticisms are only given to the prime minister but not ministers, and some to ministers but not Diet members. There are unspoken rules about this and you will not know them until you actually experience the criticism. You will know it for the first time when you are criticized.

I have also experienced something similar. By about 1990, I was already giving public lectures at large venues. In the year 1990 alone, I gave five lectures at Makuhari Messe. Even though I was giving lectures to an audience of 10,000 to 20,000 people, no media outlets reported on them, including newspapers, TV stations, and weekly magazines. I thought the mass media were mocking and disregarding religions as a whole. But one morning, I was suddenly met by four photographers from a magazine called *Focus* of Shinchosha Publishing Company, who were waiting to take pictures of me. They took many pictures and published a critical article. Back then, I was living in a rented house that only had one entrance. To leave the house, I had to walk down a long, narrow pathway from the door to the gate outside, and if the photographers were waiting for me at the gate, there was no way for me to escape. So, I immediately moved out of the house to an apartment near Takadanobaba Station, at the back of the Faculty of Science and Engineering at Waseda University. I lived there secretly for eight months and never left the apartment other than for work. I fled from my former house as if fleeing from loan sharks and locked myself inside the new apartment for eight months. When I went to work, I prepared two cars, which left the apartment in different directions so that I could avoid being followed. Just when I thought the world was ignoring us, we suddenly became the center of attention. It was the first time I experienced this.

In 1991, Happy Science was officially approved as a religious organization. That was the year we held a lecture event at the Tokyo Dome for the first time. At that time, many media outlets suddenly started to write critical articles about me. I reacted to some of them and ignored others. It was the start of a long fight, like the Ten Years' War. Now that more than 30 years have passed, things have calmed down overall. As more people from new generations have joined Happy Science, I think fewer people know about the struggles we went through.

Becoming the target of criticism means you have become well-known as a public figure. However, there are two kinds of criticisms: ones that should be accepted as a public figure and ones that need to be fought back because they are made based on sheer fabrications or fake information. You need to be able to differentiate between the two. As you develop yourself and your social standing rises, people will treat you differently. So, you must understand where you stand in society by observing the comments and criticisms others throw at you.

Success always comes with a price; where there is light, there is a shadow. It is difficult to shine brilliantly without casting a shadow. So, being under a spotlight means you will also cast a shadow. Not being in the spotlight means you are not yet successful, and during such times, your frustration tends to build up. But when you are in the spotlight, this time a shadow will form. People will start focusing on your negative points and criticizing you. You will even be criticized for things that others are not. A lot of fake information about you will also circulate. But how much you can bear this hardship will show your caliber as a person.

It is difficult to continuously succeed in a true sense as a human being. You need to make efforts year after year, and even if you have succeeded, you need to be careful not to fall from grace in your twilight years. For example, company owners cannot let their guard down even when they reach the age of 65 or older. They need to make sure that their business does not fail, as they will never know when their company will go into the red, go bankrupt, or become involved in a scandal. Sometimes, a tax office may investigate the company and claim that it is evading taxes. As society goes through changes, its systems can also change, so it is very difficult to keep winning and be successful for decades.

I have been teaching Invincible Thinking since the early days of Happy Science when I was about 32 years old. Indeed, it is difficult to keep winning and be successful. Even so, strive to win when you can, and when you fail, learn lessons from your experiences and rise again. What is important is that you learn lessons from your failures, make sure not to repeat the same mistakes, and think about how to turn those lessons into seeds of success. These are the kinds of efforts you need to make. I taught this philosophy at a relatively young age when I was 32. About 30 years have passed since then and I still abide by the same philosophy.

What is different now is that after having accumulated decades of experience in my career, I have gotten faster at dealing with issues and solving them. I can now recover quickly from events that would have caused me great damage when I was young, or that I would have considered failures, in the same way that a tilted ship quickly regains balance. I have also become quicker at detecting dangers or risks in advance.

6

Awaken to Eternal Life to Liberate Yourself from the World of Suffering

As long as you are living as a human, you will face criticism and make mistakes

Before closing this lecture, let me tell you one more thing. It is impossible to live in this world and be completely free from negative assessments or remarks, or any mistakes at all. As long as you are living as a human, you can never escape them. So, even if you fail, are criticized, or are bad-mouthed, take it to mean that it is a chance for you to reflect on yourself. Accept the comments that will benefit you, but do not take the spiteful ones to heart. If other people are spiteful toward you based on misunderstandings, pray for them so they will not fall to hell. In such cases, all you can do is pray with good intentions that they will stop walking the wrong path and return to heaven. Those who fall to hell regardless will learn their lessons in a suitable place in hell.

This year [2022], I intend to give a more detailed explanation about how and in what kind of world Punishers are giving punishments to the spirits. People need to learn more about these kinds of truths. How you have lived in this world will be judged by Yama [the Special Judge of Hell] in the afterlife and those who lived in the wrong way will be sent to an appropriate place in hell and be made to self-reflect under the Punishers. Just as I said at the beginning of the lecture, some people may make fun of these stories and think, "I want to live the way I want. As long as I'm happy now, I'm OK. I'm satisfied with what I do, so what's wrong with that? I won't listen to what other people have to say." But what awaits these people after death is a long period of self-reflection.

As it is taught in Buddhism, the world of suffering is a reality that exists. To escape from it, you must awaken to the fact that your real entity is an eternal soul and that you will continue to exist eternally as a soul. You must know that your existence will not perish after death. No matter how far materialism spreads or science advances in this world, your life will not perish and your soul will live on. Whether you will go to heaven or hell after death, or to which part of heaven you will go, is determined by how you live on earth—a training ground for souls. People who are full of pride and always boast about themselves will return to the place called the *Tengu* [long-nosed goblins] Realm. Those who commit wrongdoings in hiding and trick or deceive others for self-gain, but are not bad enough to be doomed to hell, will usually return to the *Yokai* [monsters and goblins] Realm. Those who skillfully lure people of the opposite sex will return to the *Youma* [bewitching spirits] Realm.

On the other hand, those of utmost evil who deserve punishment will fall to the deepest part of hell called the Abysmal Hell. Scholars, authors, actors, singers, and other famous figures have also fallen there. Those who polluted other people's minds while they were alive will be isolated and confined to a place from which they cannot escape. They will fall as if falling straight into the pit of a well. They will not be able to escape or meet other spirits in hell. There are many other spirits in hell, but because those in the Abysmal Hell are ideological criminals, they are not allowed to meet or interact with other spirits. Some spirits have been isolated there for hundreds of years. As they inhabit there for a long time, their bodies will transform and take the appearance of a devil. Some of them manage to get out of there, become the kings of hell, demon kings, or devils, and start to control others. There are different levels to evil spirits and some of them use minions to commit evil. They target a living person who is as powerful as they are and plot to drag that person into hell. They are always on the lookout for a target among the living. Sometimes, a fight will break out between these evil beings and angels.

In the world of suffering, choose to live the way God wishes

In this way, we are living in an eternal world. If you think about your future or how you could end up after death, you will know how you should live in this world. This world may seem like a world of suffering, but despite this, you need to consider what kind of life God wishes you to live and choose to live that way. This is important.

Here is a simple way to tell whether your current state of mind is attuned to heaven or hell. Those who always blame other people, the environment, or society for things that do not go well are more likely to go to hell. Those who feel responsible for their failures, think about what they could have done better, and make efforts to improve themselves are more likely to go to heaven. Although this is a rough way to put it, it is true. You can tell which world you are likely to go to by looking at your mentality.

Despite living in the same circumstances, some people live in gratitude while others live with grumbles and complaints. Because some spirits are ignorant of this simple truth, they suffer for hundreds or thousands of years in hell, which is very sad.

Moreover, not only should you admit your mistakes, but you must also give thanks to those who helped you or guided you and return their favor. This attitude will surely bring you victory in life. Therefore, please do not blame other people or the environment but, instead, have gratitude for those who helped you or guided you and think about returning the favors you received from them back to society and contributing to your country and the world. It is important to have these attitudes.

You cannot eliminate the world of suffering completely from earth, nor can you escape entirely from the world of suffering while you are living on earth. But if you turn your attention toward how you should live as a soul with eternal life and face the challenges squarely, you will come to realize that you are the one who must carve out your own life. This realization will liberate you from the world of suffering.

Today, I spoke on the topic of the world of suffering. I hope it will be of some help to you.

CHAPTER THREE

Searching for the Starting Point of Enlightenment

—The lifestyle that will decide whether you go to heaven or hell

Originally recorded in Japanese on April 6, 2008
at Nara Local Temple in Nara, Japan.
English translation.

1

The Essential Points of Enlightenment

Enlightenment starts with knowing who you are

Today's lecture will be my 19th one this year [2008]. Out of the 19, six were English lectures. I have been making my rounds [to various places around the world], but I am often the one getting encouraged by the Happy Science believers who come to the lecture instead.

When I gave a lecture at San Francisco Temple the other day (refer to *On Happiness* [Tokyo: Happy Science, 2021]), there was a family who drove 2,500 kilometers [about 1,550 miles] all the way from Calgary, Canada to listen to my lecture. It took them two days to get there by car. After listening to my hour-long lecture, they spent another two days driving back home. Hearing this moved me to tears. They must have come to my lecture thinking, "This will be our first and last opportunity to attend in person."

I, myself, flew halfway across the globe to give the lecture, so in that sense, we both made an effort. However, this is my profession and it is my job to make the trip. This family, on the contrary, drove 2,500 kilometers to listen to my hour-long lecture spoken in what was probably poor English. I heard about this the day before the lecture while they were actually on their way to the temple. I remember feeling truly grateful and sorry at the same time, and I once again thought, "I must say something meaningful, even just a line or two," which is something I always keep in mind when I give a lecture in Japan.

In the same lecture, there was someone from Eastern Europe who asked me, "When do you plan to give a lecture in Budapest or Warsaw?" The question took me by surprise, but I knew I should not say, "I do not have any plans," so I said, "Hmm, within the next five to 10 years." She seemed disappointed by that answer regardless, so I added, "We are currently expanding our International Division (now International Headquarters), so please be patient." I felt sorry because that was all I could say.

I want to use the technique of *bunshin-no-jyutsu* [shadow-cloning technique] to give guidance in different places at the same time, but it is impossible as long as I am in a physical body. I can as a spirit, but I cannot in a physical body because it limits me. To overcome this, I intend to use anything I can, such as satellite broadcasting via radio waves, to preach the Truth.

Ideally, I would like to visit each of the Happy Science branches and give a talk. But since there are so many, there is a possibility that I will not complete my "pilgrimage around the world" unlike those of you who admirably complete your *ohyakudo-mairi* [a form of pilgrimage where people visit shrines and temples 100 times to make a prayer]. So I am hoping that people will forgive me for using satellite broadcasting as an alternative method. That way, I can say "I visited you in spirit."

Of course, I would like to visit each location in person and speak directly to the people there. In the last 10 years, I have not been able to meet you all in person (at the time of the lecture). So, I suspect that you feel somewhat sad because you may not have met me, the master, directly even though you are a believer. I truly regret this myself.

I should essentially be guiding you myself. I understand that it is difficult for a believer to fully grasp that he or she is a follower if one has never heard the master speak in person. I understand how it feels, so I think it is a good idea to listen to my lecture directly at least once.

The title of today's lecture was initially "Be an Indomitable Believer." It was set by our General Headquarters to accommodate the audience watching through live broadcasts nationwide. But after coming to Nara, I had a second thought about the title yesterday and concluded that the lecture title was not suitable for this place.

Today, I wore these "deer-colored clothes" [*while holding the collars of his light-brown suit with both hands*] and came in a full deer-look-a-like outfit. Now is a good season to go sightseeing, so I was feeling relaxed and hoping to visit the mountain and see cherry blossoms and deer, as well as the Great Buddha Statue. However, the plans changed, and this lecture ended up being broadcast live to a much wider area.

Even so, I felt that Nara was not a good place to give a pep talk. This is the place where Japanese Buddhism started, so a more appropriate topic would be something along the lines of "the starting point of Buddhism" or "the starting point of enlightenment." That is why I came up with the title, "Searching for the Starting Point of Enlightenment" and told our staff this at around 8:30 this morning. Despite the last-minute change, the monitors [screened to the audience before the lecture] displayed the new title and I was impressed by how quickly our staff responded. Happy Science staff are, indeed, amazing; they are quite hardworking. I was surprised to see that the title had already been updated.

So today, I would like to talk about the starting point of enlightenment in simple terms. It would be unkind of me to simply say, "You can learn about it by reading all of my books," so I will explain it in a way that is easy to understand even for newcomers to Happy Science and young children.

What is most important when it comes to attaining enlightenment? Let me zero in on this point deeply. First, it is important to discover who you are and what you are. When you think about who you are, you may immediately think of the physical self, because that is what everyone else sees as you. But the truth is, you also have a spiritual self or a spirit body that takes the exact same form as your physical body and is dwelling inside it. The key question is whether you can believe this or not. You could call it a "spirit," "spirit body," "soul," or even a "mind." Regardless of what you call it, this spiritual self, which is invisible to the eyes, overlaps your physical body. So you are a dual existence of the two. Whether or not you can acknowledge, be aware of, or accept this truth is the fundamental point of enlightenment. In a sense, this is an important point that divides humans into two types of people.

Buddhism teaches you to value your imperishable nature and not be attached to the physical body

Even though society has become more modernized through scientific development, it has regressed in a spiritual sense. With rapid advancements in the study of the physical body and material things, people have become more materialistic and turned their attention to the physical aspects of life. As science has progressed and technology has become more advanced, people now think that religion is old-fashioned and they have become reluctant to speak about spiritual matters.

In Japan, after World War II ended, the university professors of Buddhist or religious studies began to find it embarrassing to write about spirits and souls because it would sound superstitious. This was perhaps partly because of Japan's defeat in the war. It became trendy to interpret Buddhism materialistically and say, "Shakyamuni Buddha taught that human bodies will eventually perish in the same way that mud houses will be washed away by the flooding of the Ganges." But this idea is based on materialism.

Buddha, indeed, used a metaphor like this to teach people that physical bodies will eventually perish, but think about it: Buddhism would not have lasted 2,500 years just by teaching something so obvious, that is, that mud houses would be washed away in a flood. Do you not think so? Many houses in India are made of mud because bricks are expensive, so whenever there is a flood, the mud houses get washed away. If you call this enlightenment, most people will say, "No way. That is obvious." Buddhism is not based on the mere idea that "Houses made of reinforced concrete will not be washed away but houses made of mud will be." Understanding this idea is by no means enlightenment. The true meaning behind this metaphor is that no matter how strongly you are attached to your physical body, it will eventually perish like the mud house; therefore, it is important to value the part of you that is imperishable and to see it as your true self. This is the true teaching of Buddhism. It is as simple as that.

Modern Buddhism teaches the exact opposite of what Shakyamuni taught

The truth is that simple, but those who are considered eminent or prominent professors of Buddhist or religious studies still do not understand it. The honorary professors and presidents of Buddhist universities are saying things like, "Everything ends with death. The soul is merely a superstition. Even Shakyamuni Buddha himself denied its existence and said that everything ends when the physical body perishes. So, Buddhism is all about materialism." Given that Buddhist studies have strayed this far from the truth, I feel that Buddhism is now in its last days—it is coming to an end.

Christianity also has an aspect that denies spiritual matters, and that is because those who preach at churches have become mediocre, salaried workers. If they were true religious leaders, they should not be able to go without sensing spiritual matters.

The same is true with full-time Buddhist monks. Even the heads of Buddhist temples openly say that they do not know what happens after death. When asked whether souls exist or where we will go after death, they just reply, "I do not know." They cannot give answers and instead say, "I was taught by my teachers at a Buddhist university that there is no soul. I passed my exam and earned my qualification as a monk by writing that everything ends with death." However, what they learned is the exact opposite of the truth. It is completely opposite of the true teachings.

This is why a new Buddhism is greatly in need and must be taught. Modern Buddhism [that denies spiritual matters] is mistaken and it has gone too far in spreading wrong ideas; this is unforgivable. Instead of using difficult words from classical scriptures, we need to give teachings in the modern language that is spoken today so people can easily understand them.

2

The Starting Point of Enlightenment (1): Being Aware that Humans Are Spiritual Beings

The most crucial point of enlightenment is being aware that humans are spiritual beings

The first element of the starting point of enlightenment is to be aware that humans are spiritual beings. People who have awakened to this Truth have awakened to the first element of the starting point of enlightenment.

Even among you Happy Science believers, how many of you are 100 percent certain that humans are spiritual beings? Some of you may say, "Over 50 percent certain," while others may say, "60 percent" or "80 percent." Some of you may say, "I am 99 percent sure, but I can't decide on the remaining one percent until after I die." But I have been fighting for more than 20 years to prove that it is 100 percent true. In these 20-plus years, I have published hundreds of books and given numerous lectures (over

3,200 books and 3,500 lectures as of January 2025). People who work closely with me have also witnessed many spiritual phenomena, so for me as well as for them, there is no room for doubt. This is the most crucial point of enlightenment.

So, experts in Buddhist philosophy who misinterpret Buddhism and claim that everything ends with death, or that Shakyamuni Buddha's teachings are based on materialism, are all frauds, though I may sound harsh. My advice to them is, "Please do not say anything. If you keep silent, you will have a higher chance of going to heaven. But if you continuously teach these wrong ideas, you will be in serious trouble later on. Teaching false ideas that go against the Truth will bring you great suffering in the other world."

Let me say it again. Being aware that humans are spiritual beings is the first essential point of enlightenment. You can deepen your spiritual awareness by practicing meditations at Happy Science shojas [facilities for prayer and spiritual training]. Some of our believers have experienced spiritual phenomena, for instance, seen a spiritual being or heard the voice of their guardian spirit. Spirituality is crucial when seeking enlightenment.

Do not trust famous scholars and Buddhist experts who deny the spirit

No matter how famous a scholar or Buddhist expert may be, he is wrong to say, "There is no such thing as a spirit. There is no such thing as the other world. Everything ends with death." Never believe this kind of statement. It is a matter of right or wrong, like choosing between heads and tails on a coin; there is no middle ground. These scholars and monks look into Buddha's teachings and select only the parts that can be interpreted to support materialism. Then they piece them together to elaborate their own theory. But what they select is only a small portion of teachings from the vast amount of Buddha's teachings.

Buddhist sutras contain a large number of descriptions that acknowledge the existence of spiritual beings. If you read the sutras yourself, you will find many passages that mention spiritual beings—they can be found in many different places. Shakyamuni Buddha acknowledged the existence of gods, or high spirits as we call them in Happy Science. Many gods are mentioned in Buddhist sutras. Demons are also depicted. But scholars and monks regard them as mere symbols of mental delusion and interpret them in the context of modern notions of common sense. The truth is that these depictions are based on true stories—they are all a reality. I myself have had similar experiences to those that Shakyamuni Buddha had. So, the first and essential point of enlightenment is to be aware that humans are spiritual beings.

3

The Starting Point of Enlightenment (2): Knowing that Your Mindset Will Determine Your Destination in the Afterlife

The current state of your mind tells you where you will go after death

The second element of the starting point of enlightenment is to know the following truth: "Just as there are heaven and hell in the other world, there is a heavenly and a hellish way of life in this world in a spiritual sense. Put simply, whether you will go to heaven or hell in the afterlife is already determined by the state of mind you have in this world." This is a typical idea in Buddhism, which differentiates Buddhism from Christianity.

Your state of mind or what you are thinking now, in other words, the level of your enlightenment will strictly determine where you will go after death. What this means is that if your mind is hellish now and you die now, you will fall to hell, and if your mind is heavenly now and you die now, you will go to heaven. In the same way, if you have the mind of a bodhisattva, you will return to the Bodhisattva Realm. So, the current state of your mind corresponds to the world you will go to after death. In this way, this world and the other world perfectly correlate with each other.

For this reason, Happy Science encourages people to attain happiness that can be carried over from this world to the other world. This is the essence of Buddhist teachings. It is why we always teach people to seek a good, correct way of life.

Evil spirits possess the living because they want to save themselves

When teaching good and evil, we often mention bad spirits, such as demons, devils, malicious spirits, and vengeful ghosts. This is because they really do exist. Many people have either seen these beings or had experiences with them. Only a small number of people have actually met or spoken with angels, but you can easily find people who have had negative spiritual experiences with evil spirits. This is because hell is located closer to this third dimensional world. Because people who live in a worldly way tend to have similar thoughts to those of the spirits in hell, their minds are likely to be attuned more to the world of hell.

When I first experienced spiritual phenomena and began to communicate with spirits, what shocked me the most was that evil spirits really exist. I can hardly believe that these spirits were once humans. They have turned into quite pitiful beings after death. They are so miserable that I can only feel sorry for them. Many of them seem to have been respectable individuals while alive; they were well dressed, wealthy, highly educated, or held a high social status such as company manager or president. Nonetheless, they are now suffering in hell and all they can think about is getting help.

They are in the same state as someone drowning in the ocean. People who are drowning will desperately scream for help. They just want to be saved; that is all they wish for themselves. In the same way, spirits in hell are desperate for help, so with the hopes of being saved, they possess anyone they find.

If you recall the movie *Titanic*, there was a scene where half the people on the cruise ship were thrown into the frigid sea as there were not enough lifeboats to carry them all. They were struggling to stay afloat, waiting for help, but eventually froze or drowned to death. In a situation like that, people will grab anything they can to save themselves. Many of the first-class passengers survived by escaping on lifeboats, but except for the people on one lifeboat, they all refused to go back and rescue the others. If they did, the people drowning in the ocean would all gather and grab onto the boat, and possibly capsize it. This would put the lives of those already on the lifeboat in jeopardy, which was why they refused to go back. They were afraid that they, too, would suffer the same fate.

Those who have fallen to hell and become lost souls after death are in a very similar state to the people drowning in the ocean. They are only thinking about how to save themselves, so they try hard to possess people living on earth. In other words, they are trying hard to possess "the survivors on the boat." But this will only cause the boat to capsize and drag everyone on it into the ocean. This is the spiritual reason behind a series of misfortunes that can occur within a particular household.

Righteous religions teach how to get out of hell

Recently, Japan's Ministry of Economy, Trade and Industry imposed administrative punishment on a suspicious religious group, or pseudo-religious group (at the time of the lecture). This group threatened its members and extorted money from them by saying that they would go to hell if they did not make donations. What the group did was certainly wrong, but what it said—that heaven and hell exist and that those who fall to hell will suffer there— is not wrong; it is absolutely true. This is a fundamental Truth on which religions must never compromise.

If hell did not exist, humans would have no sins and would not need to be saved. Consequently, there would be no need for any religious activity to save them. But as I said earlier, many people are suffering as if they are drowning in the ocean. When people who believed in materialism or who mocked religion die and unexpectedly become spiritual beings, they are tormented in pitch darkness, the Hell of Agonizing Cries, or other places with things like burning flames. At that time, all they can think about is how to save themselves, but because they have no knowledge of the Truth, they have no idea how to do this.

If people study the Truth in a righteous religion, they will know how to get out of hell. That is why religious facilities such as churches and temples exist in this world. So religions need to teach and guide people while they are alive. Even after they die, religions offer memorial services or prayers, like throwing down a "rope" to save them. These are the reasons we need religion in this world. In the long history of humankind, religion has not once ceased to exist. Even in communist and materialistic countries, religious activities have continued underground. The reason religions have not disappeared is that they teach us the Truth and the reality of the world. While humans can list many logical reasons to deny religion, the truth is the truth, and a fact is a fact; the Truth is unchangeable and it has always been this way since ancient times.

Thus, the first step to enlightenment is to be aware that humans are spiritual beings; the second is to know the good and evil ways for a soul to live in this world.

4

The Three Poisons of the Mind that Will Lead You to Hell

Checkpoints for returning to heaven: greed, anger, and ignorance

We must now explore what is good and what is evil. Some of you may be in a rush and say, "You teach about heaven and hell, but tell me simply how I can avoid going to hell and go to heaven instead. That's all I need to know; I don't need any other teachings. Just give me the short answer."

So, here are the simple criteria you can use to check whether you will go to heaven or hell. Be all eyes and ears and listen to me carefully. This knowledge alone may enable you to grab onto the lifeboat and avoid falling to hell. The checkpoints that Buddhism mainly teaches are the Three Poisons of the Mind, namely, greed, anger, and ignorance. The Japanese characters [*kanji*] for them are so difficult that young people nowadays probably cannot write them. I assume these characters do not even appear as a suggestion when you type them into a computer, either.

Greed: craving more than you deserve

Greed means excessive desire. This is something that people cannot see for themselves. It is hard to tell whether you, yourself, are greedy or not, but easy when it comes to other people. Everyone can see it. Ninety-nine percent of the time, people can tell when someone is greedy or has an extremely strong desire. It may be hard to tell if a person hides it well, but you can usually tell when someone is greedy.

Being greedy means craving more than you deserve. A greedy person wants more than what they are worthy of, which can mean more money, higher status, or a better reputation than they deserve. Whether or not you are craving more than you deserve is very difficult to assess for yourself, but easier in the eyes of others. To be able to determine this for yourself, you need to have an honest view of yourself and listen to what others say about you with an open mind. You cannot see it if you are self-centered.

Popular success theories prevailing today introduce many different ideas, but they often work to amplify people's greed. Essentially, we must be content with what we deserve. There is nothing wrong with reaping fruits that are in proportion to the efforts you made. If your income, position at work, status, or respect from other people is worthy of the effort you made, then there is nothing wrong with that. Receiving a high assessment as a result of a job well done is a natural consequence; it does not make you greedy. You can say that this is just and fair treatment. On the contrary, if you attempt to gain more recognition by using underhand methods—for instance, by bribing or setting a trap to bring others down—then you are greedy.

Being greedy is a method of going to hell, although this expression may give the wrong impression. Calling it the "royal road" to hell is also inappropriate. However, it is true to say that greed is the main road to hell—like a hundred-meter-wide road where many people can run. It is the main reason people end up there. Excessive desires will make you a typical greedy old man or old woman, like the ones who appear in old folktales; they will lead you to hell in the afterlife.

Anger: an animalistic desire for self-preservation

The second of the Three Poisons of the Mind is anger or rage. This is also difficult to write in *kanji*. I believe almost everyone has had the experience of losing their temper. When you live on instincts, you are quick to get angry. As you live in this world, you will encounter many frustrating situations and irritating people. If the world were full of people who only praised you, then there would be no reason for you to get angry. But you hardly ever meet people like that. This is because it is much easier to criticize others than to praise them. While it is difficult to praise others, it is easy to disparage, insult, or speak ill of them. Everyone can do this without being taught; it does not take much effort to say negative things.

If people just act on their instincts, they will shower others with negative remarks. The people on the receiving end will then try to defend themselves. This desire to defend yourself is an instinct to protect yourself, which will in turn make you angry and aggressive toward other people. This feeling is somewhat understandable. It is only natural for you to want to punch someone back when they punch you. However, this anger stems from your animalistic nature. We all have a kind of animalistic nature or an instinct for self-preservation. Within self-preservation exists a kind of self-love. So, when you are in a rage, you are trying to protect yourself and are just reacting like an animal. There is this aspect to anger.

Look at animals. They are quick to get angry. Dogs get angry quickly, and so do cats. When cats are in a rage, they attempt to attack their aggressors with their tails straight up and their fur bristling. Despite being as small as they are, they still express anger to scare off dogs, for example. The moment a dog shows a sign of weakness, a cat will swiftly scramble up a nearby wall to escape. So, both dogs and cats get angry. Every animal has this aspect; they live in constant fear and anger. In other words, they live with the fear of death. They react with anger because they fear being preyed on and killed at any given moment.

Perseverance, a broad mind, and tolerance are needed to maintain peace of mind

Human society can turn into a world of animals and be filled with anger if we leave it to take its natural course. That being said, humans also have an instinct to get closer to God or Buddha. Since we were born as humans, we need to strive to bring peace to the world as well as to our minds. This means it is all the more important to hold back our anger. We need to pursue serenity within or peace of mind. We need to know that having peace of mind is a state of happiness itself. This is something simple yet difficult to fully come to terms with.

When your mind is filled with hatred, you are far from happy. When you see a person who is full of hatred toward someone, do they look happy to you? I doubt it. The same is true of people at war. People of different ethnic groups or countries fighting in a war certainly look unhappy. That is why we want to realize peace. We must strive to create a world in which countries can determine their borders peacefully through talks. The ideal society is one where people can live in harmony with each other by accepting each other, their differences, and their ideologies. This is what we want to aim for. The same can be said on an individual level. Since people all have different characters, it is impossible to make everyone be the way you want them to be.

You need to make efforts to guide others in a better direction, but if you only accept people who listen to you and punish or destroy those who do not, then you are wrong. That would be the same as the Jewish Holocaust. There are plenty of people who may irritate you or disobey you, but how peacefully can you deal with these people and patiently guide them in a better direction? To do so requires perseverance. You need to have a lot of perseverance.

The same is true with family issues, which are often a matter of perseverance. You need endurance and a broad mind. Unless you strive to cultivate the virtues of perseverance, broadmindedness, and tolerance, you cannot maintain peace in your mind.

Therefore, it is important that you control your anger as much as possible and pursue peace of mind. In a way, the pursuit of a peaceful mind leads to the pursuit of enlightenment. And when everyone attains a peaceful mind, this world naturally becomes a beautiful place. This is my explanation of anger in the Three Poisons of the Mind.

Ignorance: the foolishness of not knowing Buddha's Truth

In the Three Poisons of the Mind, ignorance means foolishness or, to be direct, the foolishness of people who do not know Buddha's Truth.

I believe many believers of Happy Science study Buddha's Truth ardently. When they see this world through the eyes of the Truth, they probably find that many people are ignorant of the Truth and that they are conceited. Many people in the world have become *tengu* or conceited. They boast about having graduated from elite universities, being elite employees at elite companies, having a large income or making lots of money, living in big houses, being landowners, or being aristocrats— although there are no official aristocrats in Japan today. There are plenty of arrogant people in this world.

However, in the eyes of people who *do* know the Truth, people who *do not* know the Truth appear very miserable. They feel pity seeing how these ignorant people are living. This state of not knowing the Truth is what I mean by foolishness, or ignorance, in the Three Poisons of the Mind.

No matter how important the person may be in this world, it is sad if they live their life without knowing the Truth. There are well-respected people in the field of science such as astronautical engineers, theoretical physicists, planetary scientists, geophysicists, and computer scientists. Compared with these experts, people in general, including myself, cannot build a single space shuttle. Nor do the majority of people know how images are displayed on a TV screen. You could ask employees of electrical appliance manufacturers such as Sony or Panasonic, but even they probably do not know. They may only know about the components they are in charge of and not the overall process of how images are produced on a screen. It is true that this kind of professional knowledge is contributing to developing the modern world. However, it is, indeed, sad if these intelligent people do not know the important Truth that even people in the primitive ages knew.

A time will certainly come, years or decades later, when people have to pay the price of not knowing the Truth; they will have to make up for the lives they lived without knowing the Truth. They will be made to pay for the price themselves. It will come in the form of a journey through the world of hell. In most cases, people's minds are attuned to different realms of hell, so they will go through and experience each one of them. They will have to learn their lessons in each realm before they can graduate from the world of hell.

Some people use violence, tell lies, or kill others, but these actions all stem from the mind. People who did not learn about the mind will have to face repercussions by staying in hell until they know enough. The length of time it takes them to understand their mistakes will determine the length of their stay in hell.

5

Light the Candle in the Mind of Every Person

The act of scolding someone is justifiable anger and an act of love

As I explained above, the Three Poisons of the Mind are greed, anger, and ignorance. If you have thoroughly deepened your understanding of these three elements and learned to skillfully control your mind, you can say that you have attained a beginner's level of enlightenment. So first, avoid desiring more than you deserve, and second, avoid animalistic or unreasonable anger.

That being said, of course, there is justifiable anger. Justifiable anger could mean, for example, a police officer finding a thief and angrily chasing after him. It would be wrong to allow robbery saying, "Thieves are fellow humans, so they have a right to do whatever they want. Let them rob a bank if that is what they want to do." This is not right by all means.

Another form of necessary anger may be a doctor reprimanding irresponsible patients. The same is true of teachers making a stern face and scolding children who are misbehaving or telling lazy students to study harder. These cases are not acts of anger but acts of scolding, which is actually a form of love. Scolding is different from anger. Sometimes, you need to scold people to nurture them. But in most cases, people's anger is instinctive and this type of anger needs to be controlled.

The importance of telling the Truth to the people who are living in darkness

Thirdly, please live by the Truth. Those without the knowledge of the Truth are living as if they are groping in the dark, trying to find their way. They are much like people looking for a candle during a power outage caused by an earthquake, thunderstorm, or hurricane. In the eyes of those who know the Truth, people who live in ignorance seem to be living without the lights on. They are pitiful people who are struggling to find their way in the dark. That is why we must tell these people, "Light your candle. Hold it up to illuminate the room and look around." This is our missionary work. Missionary work is the act of lighting the candle in every person; it is an extremely important activity.

Many people are actually living in darkness. The world may look bright and beautiful, but in reality, the majority of people are living in darkness—namely, ignorance. Over six billion people are living in the world now (at the time of the lecture), and a few billion of them are living in ignorance. They are groping around in the dark without a light. They mistakenly believe that they are true elites, impressively successful people, or great teachers who can lecture others, when in fact they are groping in darkness and are lost. Many people are living with misconceptions of themselves like this. That is why we need to share the light from our candle and tell them, "Here, use it to light the candle of your mind."

It is truly pitiful to die without ever knowing the Truth. As you carry out your missionary work, you may sometimes encounter people who refuse to listen to the Truth. Many people just cannot accept the Truth, much like how a body covered in oil repels water. I cannot help but feel pity for them; nothing goes into them. It is as if they are covered in full armor—not a single Truth strikes a chord in their hearts.

However, as people live in this world, they are made to experience different kinds of hardships, troubles, disasters, and suffering, including misfortunes in their families. These moments are actually chances for them to awaken to the Truth. In many cases, people realize in hindsight that incidents that seemed like suffering in this world were opportunities for them to be guided to the Truth.

Therefore, even if the person you are trying to help does not understand the Truth now, tell yourself that the time is not ripe yet. Wait for the right moment for them to awaken to the Truth and continue to provide them with opportunities. A book of Truth that you offered someone may strike a chord in their heart in 10 or 20 years, even if it is not meaningful to them right now. A person you try to help out of pure love may refuse your help and just ridicule you. However, the same person may awaken to the Truth 30 years down the road.

Some people may do well themselves but their children could be met with misfortune, for example, a bad incident or an accident. At such times, they may awaken to the religious truth for the first time and attain some kind of enlightenment. Some people may even awaken to the Truth after they die. So, it is extremely important to provide people with the opportunity to encounter the Truth.

Missionary work is an act of good, so be confident that you are doing something good. In this world, many people are struggling in darkness. What they are seeing is in fact a world of illusion, which is far different from reality. This world is only a temporary abode. This is what you must understand to attain a basic level of enlightenment.

The sincere wish to help others will take you to heaven

There are a few more important points that you need to know. It is considered a sin to doubt your faith or to topple someone else's faith; being conceited and puffed up with pride is also a sin; and having wrong views or evil views is yet another sin. To avoid getting into a complex discussion, I will not talk about them in detail now, but basically, as I said earlier, start by conquering the three negative tendencies of the mind—desiring more than you deserve [greed], flying into a rage [anger], and being foolish [ignorance]. By doing so, you will be able to take the first step and attain the beginner's level of enlightenment.

The fruit of these efforts is that you will be able to attain a peaceful mind and a greater sense of happiness. Then, you will surely have a pure wish to help others, even a little, or contribute to making the world a better place. When people see how you are trying to help others or make the world a better place, there will always be some who criticize you, find fault in you, or claim that you are a hypocrite. But these people have completely twisted minds, so please do not let their criticism affect you.

If you develop such pure, sincere wishes, it means you are advancing on the path to enlightenment, and you can assume that you are walking the path to heaven. This concludes my talk on "Searching for the Starting Point of Enlightenment."

For a deeper understanding of
My Visit to Hell
see other books below by Ryuho Okawa:

The Laws of Hell [New York: IRH Press, 2023]

Words to Stop You from Falling to Hell [Tokyo: HS Press, 2025]

The following book is only available at Happy Science locations. Please see the contact information on p. 174-175.

On Happiness [Tokyo: Happy Science, 2021]

ABOUT THE AUTHOR

Founder and CEO of Happy Science Group.

Ryuho Okawa was born on July 7th, 1956, in Tokushima, Japan. After graduating from the University of Tokyo with a law degree, he joined a Tokyo-based trading house. While working at its New York headquarters, he studied international finance at the Graduate Center of the City University of New York. In 1981, he attained Great Enlightenment and became aware that he is El Cantare with a mission to bring salvation to all humankind.

In 1986, he established Happy Science. It now has members in 179 countries across the world, with more than 700 branches and temples as well as 10,000 missionary houses around the world.

He has given over 3,500 lectures (of which more than 150 are in English) and published over 3,200 books (of which more than 600 are Spiritual Interview Series), and many are translated into 42 languages. Along with *The Laws of the Sun* and *The Laws of Hell*, many of the books have become best sellers or million sellers. To date, Happy Science has produced 28 movies under his supervision. He has given the original story and concept and is also the Executive Producer. He has also composed music and written lyrics of over 450 pieces.

Moreover, he is the Founder of Happy Science University and Happy Science Academy (Junior and Senior High School), Founder and President of the Happiness Realization Party, Founder and Honorary Headmaster of Happy Science Institute of Government and Management, Founder of IRH Press Co., Ltd., and the Chairperson of NEW STAR PRODUCTION Co., Ltd. and ARI Production Co., Ltd.

BOOKS BY RYUHO OKAWA

The Latest Titles

One More Step Forward

The Invincible Thinking to get you through tough times

Paperback • 256 pages • $17.95
ISBN: 978-1-958655-25-2 (May 7, 2025)

Success in life is determined not by our circumstances but by our mindset and how we think. In this book, the author reveals from his first-hand experience how the spirit of self-help can create new values.

Ryuho Okawa is a true self-made man with an indomitable spirit to bring happiness to all humankind. His drive to keep moving forward by taking steady steps through the power of discipline has led to the publication of over 3,200 books in just 37 years. Unlock the keys to lifelong growth and success by reading this book.

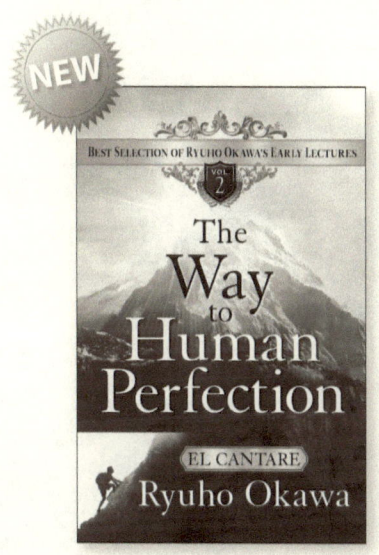

The Way to Human Perfection

Best Selection of Ryuho Okawa's Early Lectures (Volume 2)

Paperback • 200 pages • $17.95
ISBN: 978-1-958655-20-7 (Oct. 22, 2024)

The path to enlightenment starts from understanding 'the eternal viewpoint of life.' Through each chapter, Ryuho Okawa navigates us to shift the perspective of ourselves from a 'finite self' living a limited life to an 'eternal self' living an eternal life.

If we can recognize that our soul is eternal and that every thought and action has consequences, then we can realize that caring and bringing joy to others are the keys to true happiness and success.

Walking the path towards higher enlightenment is the source of improving character so we can build better relationships with others. It is the new value to unlock a bright future.

Gain a Deeper Understanding of Hell and Exorcism

The Laws of Hell

"IT" follows .....

Paperback • 264 pages • $17.95
ISBN: 978-1-958655-04-7 (May 1, 2023)

Whether you believe it or not, the Spirit World and hell do exist. Currently, the Earth's population has exceeded 8 billion, and unfortunately, 1 in 2 people are falling to hell.

This book is a must-read at a time like this since more and more people are unknowingly heading to hell; the truth is, new areas of hell are being created, such as 'internet hell' and 'hell on earth.' Also, due to the widespread materialism, there is a sharp rise in the earthbound spirits wandering around Earth because they have no clue about the Spirit World.

To stop hell from spreading and to save the souls of all human beings, Ryuho Okawa has compiled vital teachings in this book. This publication marks his 3,100th book and is the one and only comprehensive Truth about the modern hell.

NEW

Words to Stop You from Falling to Hell

Paperback • 136 pages • $15.95
ISBN: 979-8887371238 (Jan. 27, 2025)

Open this book and discover the world of hell the author saw through his spiritual sight. The vivid and raw descriptions of the punishment in hell will leave you speechless. Whether you will go there is not only determined by your actions but every thought you have in your mind. You might be able to fool people, but you cannot fool God's eyes. By reading this book of salvation, reflect on your thoughts and actions for it is never too late to change your destiny.

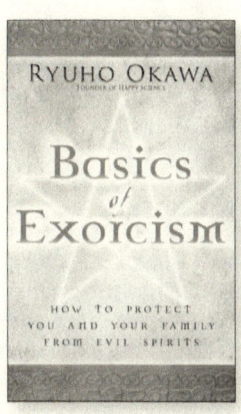

Basics of Exorcism

How to Protect You and Your Family from Evil Spirits

Paperback • 130 pages • $14.95
ISBN: 979-8887370408 (Feb. 27, 2015)

Learn about how to protect yourself and your family from the influences of evil spirits and demons. Discover the spiritual reasons for issues such as personality disorder and schizophrenia from a spiritual leader with extraordinary psychic abilities.

Spiritual World 101

A Guide to a Spiritually Happy Life

Paperback • 184 pages • $14.95
ISBN: 979-8-88737-031-6 (Mar. 25, 2015)

This book is a spiritual guidebook that will answer all your questions about the spiritual world, with illustrations and diagrams explaining your guardian spirit and the secrets of God and Buddha. By reading this book, you will be able to understand the true meaning of life and find happiness in everyday life.

"People are born into this world in order to learn something and, after they have done this, they take it back with them to the Real World, to the true world they originally came from."—Excerpt from Epilogue

My Journey through the Spirit World

A True Account of My Experiences of the Hereafter

Paperback • 224 pages • $15.95
ISBN: 978-1-942125-41-9 (Jul. 25, 2018)

What happens when we die? What is the afterworld like? Do heaven and hell really exist? This unique and authentic guide to the spirit world will awaken us to the truth of life and death, and show us how we should start living so that we can return to a bright world of heaven.

The Truth about Spiritual Phenomena

Life's Q&A with El Cantare

Paperback • 232 pages • $17.95
ISBN: 978-1-958655-0-92 (Oct. 27, 2023)

These are the records of Ryuho Okawa's answers to 26 questions related to spiritual phenomena and mental health, which were conducted live during his early public lectures with the audience. With his great spiritual ability, he revealed the unknown spiritual Truth behind the spiritual phenomena.

Buddhist Teachings for People Today

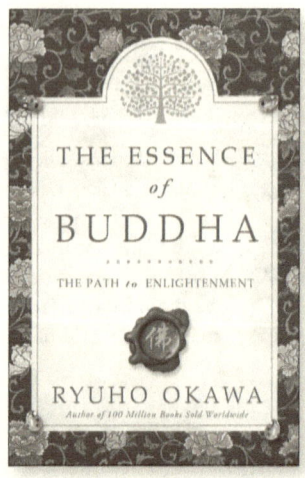

The Essence of Buddha

The Path to Enlightenment

Paperback • 208 pages • $14.95
ISBN: 978-1-942125-06-8 (Oct. 1, 2016)

In this book, Ryuho Okawa imparts in simple and accessible language his wisdom about the essence of Shakyamuni Buddha's philosophy of life and enlightenment—teachings that have been inspiring people all over the world for over 2,500 years. By offering a new perspective on core Buddhist thoughts that have long been cloaked in mystique, Okawa brings these teachings to life for modern people. *The Essence of Buddha* distills a way of life that anyone can practice to achieve a life of self-growth, compassionate living, and true happiness.

An Unshakable Mind

How to Overcome Life's Difficulties

Paperback • 180 pages • $17.95
ISBN:978-1-942125-91-4 (Nov. 15, 2023)

This book will guide you to build the genuine self-confidence necessary to shape a resilient character and withstand life's turbulence.

Ryuho Okawa breaks down the causes of life's difficulties and provides solutions to overcome them from the spiritual viewpoint of life based on the laws of the mind. As you engage further with this book, you will discover the hidden spiritual causes behind some of life's difficulties. Finding the true causes of problems makes it easier to confront, tackle and solve them.

This practical yet very insightful book is filled with powerful words of encouragement that will resonate within your soul. Let this book be your companion through life's hardships.

Recommended Books

The Laws of Great Enlightenment

Always Walk with Buddha

Paperback • 232 pages • $17.95
ISBN: 978-1-942125-62-4 (Nov. 7, 2019)

Constant self-blame for mistakes, setbacks, or failures and feelings of unforgivingness toward others are hard to overcome. Through the power of enlightenment, we can learn to forgive ourselves and others, overcome life's problems, and courageously create a brighter future ourselves. *The Laws of Great Enlightenment* addresses the core problems of life that people often struggle with and offers advice on how to overcome them based on spiritual truths.

The True Eightfold Path

Guideposts for Self-Innovation

Paperback • 256 pages • $16.95
ISBN: 978-1-942125-80-8 (Mar. 30, 2021)

Buddha's Eightfold Path is called 'The Secret Treasure of Mankind' as it has the tremendous power to transform one's life inside out to become a happier, compassionate and more productive person. Apply Okawa's 'True Eightfold Path' in today's world and live a life that is free of regret.

The Rebirth of Buddha

My Eternal Disciples, Hear My Words

Paperback • 280 pages • $17.95
ISBN: 978-1-942125-95-2 (Aug. 15, 2022)

These are the messages of Buddha who has returned to this modern age as promised to His eternal beloved disciples. They are in simple words and poetic style, yet contain profound messages. Once you start reading these passages, your soul will be replenished as the plant absorbs the water, and you will remember why you chose this era to be born into with Buddha. Listen to the voices of your Eternal Master and awaken to your calling.

The Strong Mind

The Art of Building the Inner Strength to Overcome Life's Difficulties

Paperback • 192 pages • $15.95
ISBN: 978-1-942125-36-5 (May 25, 2018)

The strong mind is what we need to rise time and again, and to move forward no matter what difficulties we face in life. This book will inspire and empower you to take courage, develop a mature and cultivated heart, and achieve resilience and hardiness so that you can break through the barriers of your limits and keep winning in the battle of your life.

The Laws Series

The Laws of the Sun, the first publication of the Laws Series, ranked in the annual best-selling list in Japan in 1994. Since then, the Laws Series' titles have ranked in the annual best-selling list every year for more than three decades, setting socio-cultural trends in Japan and around the world. The first three Laws Series are *The Laws of the Sun*, *The Golden Laws*, and *The Laws of Eternity*.

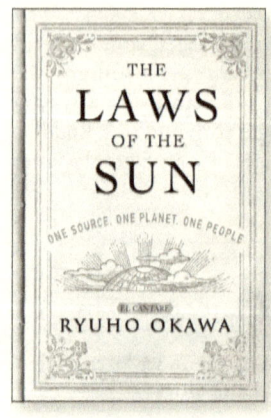

The Laws of the Sun

One Source, One Planet, One People

Paperback • 288 pages • $15.95
ISBN: 978-1-942125-43-3 (Oct. 25, 2018)

IMAGINE IF YOU COULD ASK GOD why He created this world and about the spiritual laws He used to shape us and everything around us. If we could understand His designs and intentions, we could discover what our goals in life should be and whether our actions move us closer to those goals or farther away.

At a young age, a spiritual calling prompted Ryuho Okawa to outline what he innately understood to be universal truths for all humankind. In *The Laws of the Sun*, Okawa outlines these laws of the universe and provides a road map for living one's life with greater purpose and meaning. In this powerful book, Ryuho Okawa reveals the transcendent nature of consciousness and the secrets of the multidimensional universe as well as the meaning of humans that exist within it. By understanding the different stages of love and following the Buddhist Eightfold Path, he believes we can speed up our eternal process of development. *The Laws of the Sun* shows the way to realize true happiness—a happiness that continues from this world through the other.

The Laws of Eternity

El Cantare Unveils the Structure of the Spirit World

Paperback • 224 pages • $17.95
ISBN: 978-1-958655-16-0 (May 15, 2024)

"Where do we come from and where do we go after death?"

This unparalleled book offers us complete answers to life's most important questions that we all are confronted with at some point or another. In *The Laws of Eternity*, author Ryuho Okawa takes us on a journey to the other world, a place where we came from before we were born and return to after death.

This book reveals the eternal mysteries and the ultimate secrets of Earth's spirit group that have been covered by the veil of legends and myths. Encountering the long-hidden Eternal Truths that are revealed for the first time in human history will change the way you live your life now.

WHO IS EL CANTARE?

El Cantare means "the Light of the Earth." He is the Supreme God of the Earth who has been guiding humankind since the beginning of Genesis, and He is the Creator of the universe. He is whom Jesus called Father and Muhammad called Allah and is *Ame-no-Mioya-Gami*, Japanese Father God. Different parts of El Cantare's core consciousness have descended to Earth in the past, once as Alpha and another as Elohim. His branch spirits, such as Shakyamuni Buddha and Hermes, have descended to Earth many times and helped to flourish many civilizations. To unite various religions and to integrate various fields of study in order to build a new civilization on Earth, a part of the core consciousness has descended to Earth as Master Ryuho Okawa.

Alpha is a part of the core consciousness of El Cantare who descended to Earth around 330 million years ago. Alpha preached Earth's Truths to harmonize and unify Earth-born humans and space people who came from other planets.

Elohim is a part of the core consciousness of El Cantare who descended to Earth around 150 million years ago. He gave wisdom, mainly on the differences between light and darkness, good and evil.

Ame-no-Mioya-Gami (Japanese Father God) is the Creator God and the Father God who appears in ancient literature, *Hotsuma Tsutae*. It is believed that He descended on the foothills of Mt. Fuji about 30,000 years ago and built the Fuji dynasty, which is the root of the Japanese civilization. With justice as the central pillar, Ame-no-Mioya-Gami's teachings spread to ancient civilizations of other countries in the world.

Shakyamuni Buddha was born as a prince into the Shakya clan around 2,600 years ago. When he was 29 years old, he renounced the world and sought enlightenment. He later attained Great Enlightenment and founded Buddhism.

Hermes is one of the 12 Olympian gods in Greek mythology, but the spiritual Truth is that he taught the teachings of love and progress around 4,300 years ago which became the origin of the current Western civilization. He is a hero who truly existed.

Ophealis was born in Greece around 6,500 years ago and was the leader who took an expedition to as far as Egypt. He is the God of miracles, prosperity, and arts, and is known as Osiris in Egyptian mythology.

Rient Arl Croud was born as a king of the ancient Incan Empire around 7,000 years ago and taught about the mysteries of the mind. In the heavenly world, he is responsible for the interactions that take place between various planets.

Thoth was an almighty leader who built the golden age of the Atlantic civilization around 12,000 years ago. In Egyptian mythology, he is known as God Thoth.

Ra Mu was a leader who built the golden age of the civilization of Mu around 17,000 years ago. As a religious leader and a politician, he ruled by uniting religion and politics.

ABOUT HAPPY SCIENCE

Happy Science is a religious group founded on the faith in El Cantare who is the God of the Earth, and the Creator of the universe. The essence of human beings is the soul that was created by God, and we all are children of God. God is our true parent, so in our souls, we have a fundamental desire to "believe in God, love God, and get closer to God." And, we can get closer to God by living with God's Will as our own. In Happy Science, we call this the "Exploration of Right Mind." More specifically, it means to practice the Fourfold Path, which consists of "Love, Wisdom, Self-Reflection, and Progress."

Love: Love means "love that gives," or mercy. God hopes for the happiness of all people. Therefore, living with God's Will as our own means to start by practicing "love that gives."

Wisdom: God's love is boundless. It is important to learn various Truths in order to understand the heart of God.

Self-Reflection: Once you learn the heart of God and the difference between His mind and yours, you should strive to bring your own mind closer to the mind of God—that process is called self-reflection. Self-reflection also includes meditation and prayer.

Progress: Since God hopes for the happiness of all people, you should also make progress in your love, and make an effort to realize utopia in which everyone in your society, country, and eventually all humankind can become happy.

As we practice this Fourfold Path, our souls will advance toward God step by step. That is when we can attain real happiness—our souls' desire to get closer to God comes true.

In Happy Science, we conduct activities to make ourselves happy through belief in Lord El Cantare and to spread this faith to the world and bring happiness to all. We welcome you to join our activities!

We hold events and activities to help you practice the Fourfold Path at our branches, temples, missionary centers, and missionary houses

Love: We hold various volunteering activities. Our members conduct missionary work together as the greatest practice of love.

Wisdom: We offer our comprehensive collection of books of Truth, many of which are available online and at Happy Science locations. In addition, we offer numerous opportunities such as seminars or book clubs to learn the Truth.

Self-Reflection: We offer opportunities to polish your mind through self-reflection, meditation, and prayer. Many members have experienced improvement in their human relationships by changing their own minds.

Progress: We also offer seminars to enhance your power of influence. Because it is also important to do well at work to make society better, we hold seminars to improve your work and management skills.

"The True Words Spoken By Buddha"

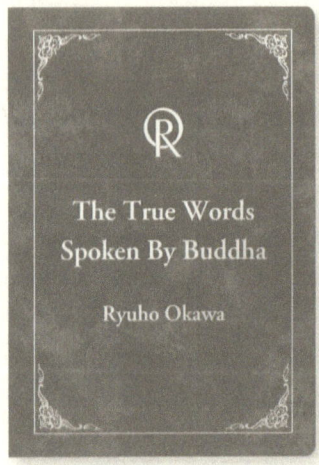

"The True Words Spoken By Buddha" is an English sutra given directly from the spirit of Shakyamuni Buddha, who is a part of Master Ryuho Okawa's subconscious. The words in this sutra are not of a mere human being but are the words of God or Buddha sent directly from the ninth dimension, which is the highest realm of the Earth's Spirit World.

"The True Words Spoken By Buddha" is an essential sutra for us to connect and live with God or Buddha's Will as our own.

MEMBERSHIPS

MEMBERSHIP

If you would like to know more about Happy Science, please consider becoming a member. Those who pledge to believe in Lord El Cantare and wish to learn more can join us.

When you become a member, you will receive the following sutras: "The True Words Spoken By Buddha," "Prayer to the Lord" and "Prayer to Guardian and Guiding Spirits."

DEVOTEE MEMBER

If you would like to learn the teachings of Happy Science and walk the path of faith, become a Devotee member who pledges devotion to the Three Treasures, which are Buddha, Dharma, and Sangha. Buddha refers to Lord El Cantare, Master Ryuho Okawa. Dharma refers to Master Ryuho Okawa's teachings. Sangha refers to Happy Science. Devoting to the Three Treasures will let your Buddha nature shine, and you will enter the path to attain true freedom of the mind.

Becoming a devotee means you become Buddha's disciple. You will discipline your mind and act to bring happiness to society.

✉ EMAIL OR **☎ PHONE CALL**
Please turn to the contact information page.

🖰 ONLINE member.happy-science.org/signup/ 🔍

CONTACT INFORMATION

Happy Science is a worldwide organization with branches and temples around the globe. For full details, visit happy-science.org. The following are some of our main Happy Science locations:

UNITED STATES AND CANADA

New York
79 Franklin St., New York, NY 10013, USA
Phone: 1-212-343-7972
Fax: 1-212-343-7973
Email: ny@happy-science.org
Website: happyscience-usa.org

New Jersey
66 Hudson St, #2R, Hoboken, NJ 07030, USA
Phone: 1-201-313-0127
Email: nj@happy-science.org
Website: happyscience-usa.org

Chicago
33 West Higgins Rd. 4040,
South Barrington, IL 60010, USA
Phone: 1-630-937-3077
Email: chicago@happy-science.org
Website: happyscience-usa.org

Florida
5208 8th St., Zephyrhills, FL 33542, USA
Phone: 1-813-715-0000
Fax: 1-813-715-0010
Email: florida@happy-science.org
Website: happyscience-usa.org

Atlanta
1874 Piedmont Ave., NE Suite 360-C
Atlanta, GA 30324, USA
Phone: 1-404-892-7770
Email: atlanta@happy-science.org
Website: happyscience-usa.org

San Francisco
525 Clinton St.
Redwood City, CA 94062, USA
Phone & Fax: 1-650-363-2777
Email: sf@happy-science.org
Website: happyscience-usa.org

Los Angeles
1590 E. Del Mar Blvd., Pasadena,
CA 91106, USA
Phone: 1-626-395-7775
Fax: 1-626-395-7776
Email: la@happy-science.org
Website: happyscience-usa.org

Orange County
16541 Gothard St. Suite 104
Huntington Beach, CA 92647
Phone: 1-714-659-1501
Email: oc@happy-science.org
Website: happyscience-usa.org

San Diego
7841 Balboa Ave. Suite #202
San Diego, CA 92111, USA
Phone: 1-626-395-7775
Fax: 1-626-395-7776
E-mail: sandiego@happy-science.org
Website: happyscience-usa.org

Hawaii
Phone: 1-808-591-9772
Fax: 1-808-591-9776
Email: hi@happy-science.org
Website: happyscience-usa.org

Kauai
3343 Kanakolu Street, Suite 5
Lihue, HI 96766, USA
Phone: 1-808-822-7007
Fax: 1-808-822-6007
Email: kauai-hi@happy-science.org
Website: happyscience-usa.org

Toronto
845 The Queensway
Etobicoke, ON M8Z 1N6, Canada
Phone: 1-416-901-3747
Email: toronto@happy-science.org
Website: happy-science.ca

Vancouver
#201-2607 East 49th Avenue,
Vancouver, BC, V5S 1J9, Canada
Phone: 1-604-437-7735
Fax: 1-604-437-7764
Email: vancouver@happy-science.org
Website: happy-science.ca

INTERNATIONAL

Tokyo
1-6-7 Togoshi, Shinagawa,
Tokyo, 142-0041, Japan
Phone: 81-3-6384-5770
Fax: 81-3-6384-5776
Email: tokyo@happy-science.org
Website: happy-science.org

London
3 Margaret St.
London, W1W 8RE United Kingdom
Phone: 44-20-7323-9255
Fax: 44-20-7323-9344
Email: eu@happy-science.org
Website: www.happyscience-uk.org

Sydney
516 Pacific Highway, Lane Cove North,
2066 NSW, Australia
Phone: 61-2-9411-2877
Fax: 61-2-9411-2822
Email: sydney@happy-science.org

Sao Paulo
Rua. Domingos de Morais 1154,
Vila Mariana, Sao Paulo SP
CEP 04010-100, Brazil
Phone: 55-11-5088-3800
Email: sp@happy-science.org
Website: happyscience.com.br

Jundiai
Rua Congo, 447, Jd. Bonfiglioli
Jundiai-CEP, 13207-340, Brazil
Phone: 55-11-4587-5952
Email: jundiai@happy-science.org

Seoul
74, Sadang-ro 27-gil,
Dongjak-gu, Seoul, Korea
Phone: 82-2-3478-8777
Fax: 82-2-3478-9777
Email: korea@happy-science.org

Taipei
No. 89, Lane 155, Dunhua N. Road,
Songshan District, Taipei City 105, Taiwan
Phone: 886-2-2719-9377
Fax: 886-2-2719-5570
Email: taiwan@happy-science.org

Taichung
No. 146, Minzu Rd., Central Dist.,
Taichung City 400001, Taiwan
Phone: 886-4-22233777
Email: taichung@happy-science.org

Kuala Lumpur
No 22A, Block 2, Jalil Link Jalan Jalil Jaya
2, Bukit Jalil 57000,
Kuala Lumpur, Malaysia
Phone: 60-3-8998-7877
Fax: 60-3-8998-7977
Email: malaysia@happy-science.org
Website: happyscience.org.my

Kathmandu
Kathmandu Metropolitan City,
Ward No. 15, Ring Road, Kimdol,
Sitapaila Kathmandu, Nepal
Phone: 977-1-537-2931
Email: nepal@happy-science.org

Kampala
Plot 877 Rubaga Road, Kampala
P.O. Box 34130 Kampala, Uganda
Email: uganda@happy-science.org

ABOUT HS PRESS

HS Press is an imprint of IRH Press Co., Ltd. IRH Press Co., Ltd., based in Tokyo, was founded in 1987 as a publishing division of Happy Science. IRH Press publishes religious and spiritual books, journals, and magazines and also operates broadcast and film production enterprises. For more information, visit *okawabooks.com*.

Follow us on:

f Facebook: Okawa Books   Instagram: OkawaBooks
Youtube: Okawa Books   Twitter: Okawa Books
Pinterest: Okawa Books   Goodreads: Ryuho Okawa

——— **NEWSLETTER** ———

To receive book-related news, promotions, and events, please subscribe to our newsletter below.

okawabooks.com/pages/subscribe

——— **AUDIO / VISUAL MEDIA** ———

YOUTUBE

PODCAST

Visit the above to learn more about Ryuho Okawa's books. Topics ranging from self-help, current affairs, spirituality, religion, and the universe.